W9-BYU-235

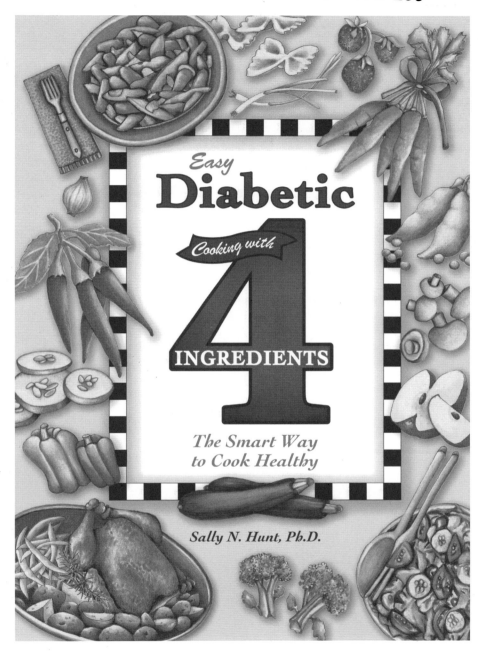

Easy
Diabetic

Cooking with

4

INGREDIENTS

*The Smart Way
to Cook Healthy*

Sally N. Hunt, Ph.D.

Diabetic Cooking
with 4 Ingredients

Copyright © 2004
By Cookbook Resources, LLC Highland Village, Texas
All rights reserved.

1st Printing   October 2004   Wire Binding
2nd Printing   September 2005 Wire Binding
3rd Printing   December 2005   Wire Binding

ISBN 1-931294-85-2
Library of Congress 2004113161

Illustrated by Nancy Murphy Griffith

Manufactured in China
Designed in the United States of America by
Cookbook Resources, LLC
541 Doubletree Drive
Highland Village, Texas 75077
Toll free 866-229-2665
www.cookbookresources.com

cookbook
resources LLC

From the Author

Caught in the rush of everyday living? Even the most health-conscious consumer would agree that healthy eating and cooking are quite a challenge! After a hard day of work, we hurry to the supermarket, grabbing familiar foods that are quick and easy to prepare, but that are probably not the healthiest food choices.

After the publication of my first book, *Easy Healthy Cooking with Four Ingredients*, I became aware of just how important easy, quick and healthy recipes are. Over and over again, people have said, "Four healthy ingredients? That's what I need!"

When I began researching nutrition requirements for diabetics, it became clear to me that the recommended foods for people with diabetes are essentially the same healthy foods everyone needs. The challenge was to develop recipes using smart, convenient products designed for people on the go, yet still be low in sugar and refined carbohydrates, sodium, fat, cholesterol and calories. Impossible? Never!

Reading food labels and looking for smart new products is a great idea, but it sometimes takes more time than we have. That hungry family waiting at home is the more urgent need, not roaming the aisles of the supermarket. I've done the research for you, providing nearly 200 smart recipes with nutritional analyses, serving sizes – even net carb counts. This cookbook takes all guesswork out of meal planning.

For the person with diabetes, the low carb dieter, or anyone short on time and long on good intentions, this cookbook is for you. *Enjoy!*

Sally N. Hunt, Ph.D. is the author of Easy Healthy Cooking with 4 Ingredients, published by Cookbook Resources, LLC, 2003, which has sold more than 10,000 copies. She has appeared on QVC Home Shopping Network and local television programs. With a Ph.D. in Home Economics, Dr. Hunt has extensive teaching experience at the college level. She is enjoying retirement in historic Natchitoches, Louisiana and plans to continue to develop creative recipes for easy, healthy cooking.

Contents

This is a great collection of recipes for everyday meals at home as well as special dishes for friends and neighbors. All dishes are delicious and packed with lots of flavors so you don't miss out anything even though you are eating "healthy". And the best part...every recipe has only 4 ingredients!

Indicates Author's Choice Recipes

10 Things to Love About This Cookbook:

10 Diabetic recipes for every taste.

9 Food exchanges and nutritional analysis for every recipe.

8 Net-carb counts per serving.

7 Smart new products.

6 Easy, step-by-step instructions.

5 Quick and easy meal ideas.

4 Familiar and "comfort" foods prepared in healthier ways.

3 Incredible desserts.

2 Every recipe has only 4 ingredients

1 Incredible desserts.

Some Smart Products Used in This Cookbook:

Bagged lettuce and mixed salad greens

Boneless skinless chicken breasts

Campbell's® Healthy Request® condensed soups

Carb Options™ Asian Teriyaki Marinade

Carb Options™ Garden Style Sauce

Carb Options™ Olive Oil Vinaigrette Dressing

Carb Options™ Original Barbecue Sauce

Carb Options™ Super Chunk Peanut Spread

Egg Beaters® egg substitute

Frozen fruit

Frozen seasoning blends

Frozen vegetable blends

Light processed cheese

Light sour cream

Light mayonnaise

Lite frozen whipped topping

Lite soy sauce

Low-carb bread

Low-carb ice cream

Low-carb whole wheat tortillas

Low-carb yogurt

Mrs. Dash® seasoning blends

Murray® Sugar Free cookies

No-salt tomato sauce

Reduced-carb pasta

Reduced-fat cheddar/mozzarella cheese

Reduced-fat cream cheese

Reduced-fat graham cracker crusts

Russell Stover® Low Carb Peanut Butter Cups

Russell Stover® Low Carb Toffee Squares

Salt-free Creole seasoning

Smart Balance® Buttery Spread

Smuckers® Natural Creamy Peanut Butter

Smuckers® Sugar Free Hot Fudge Topping™

Splenda® sugar substitute

Sugar-free fruit spreads

Sugar-free gelatin mixes

Sugar-free pudding mixes

Sugar-free maple syrup

Swanson® Natural Goodness™ Chicken Broth

Whole wheat pasta (spaghetti, rotini)

Whole wheat tortillas

Whole wheat bread, crackers

Healthy Diets for Diabetics

People with diabetes have more food choices today than ever before.

In fact, the American Diabetes Association now maintains that the diabetic diet (low in refined carbohydrates, hydrogenated fat and sodium and rich in whole grains, fruits and vegetables including beans and peas) is essentially the healthy diet recommended for anyone interested in good nutrition.

Today's smart, convenient products make healthy eating easier by eliminating refined carbohydrates, reducing fat and sodium, and adding more whole grains. The recipes in this book use many of these smart products, plus plenty of fresh vegetables, meats and fruits for every taste. Each recipe includes serving size, nutritional analysis and food exchanges plus net carbs per serving.

Without guessing, reading labels or performing calculations, you can more easily follow your doctor's recommendations for calories, carbohydrates, protein, fat and other nutrients. Use this book as a guide in meal planning for the diabetic, low-carb dieter or anyone interested in no-fuss good nutrition.

This cookbook is not intended as a substitute for the advice of a physician. Always consult your doctor and/or registered dietitian for specific instructions regarding diabetic meal plans or weight loss programs.

Nutritional information was calculated using Nutritionist Pro™ analysis software by FirstDataBank. Nutritional calculations are approximate and do not include optional ingredients, garnishes or sauces, unless specifically stated in the recipe. When two or more ingredient choices are given, the ingredient listed first is the one used in nutritional analysis. Water, non-stick cooking spray, salt substitute and pepper are counted as "free" ingredients.

Brand name products used in this cookbook are the property of their respective owners, and no claim or endorsement is implied.

Nutritional references include publications by the American Diabetes Association and American Dietetic Association, along with Understanding Nutrition, 9th Ed. 2002, Whitney, E.N. & Rolfes, S.R. Belmont, CA: Wadsworth/Thomson Learning.

What are Net Carbs?

Simply put, net carbs, as defined in this cookbook, are the result of subtracting dietary fiber content from the total carbohydrate content in one serving of a food.

For example, if a label for one serving of bread lists 7 grams of total carbohydrates and 2 grams of dietary fiber, the result would be 5 grams of net carbs in one serving of bread.

In a few recipes, sugar alcohols are also subtracted from total carbohydrate content since they are listed on product labels. Keep in mind that sugar alcohols—NOT SUGARS—are subtracted from the total carbohydrate content.

The effect of sugar alcohols on total carbohydrate intake can be significant for the carb-conscious consumer. Researchers have reported that sugar alcohols, such as maltitol and sorbitol, are not chemically broken down in the body to glucose (sugar). If sugar alcohols appear on a product's label, manufacturers are subtracting sugar alcohols from the total carbohydrates in that product, further reducing the amount of net carbs.

For a person counting daily carbohydrate intake, understanding net carbs and how they are figured may be helpful.

■ ■ ■

What are Sugar Alcohols?

Sugar alcohols provide bulk and sweetness in chewing gums, candies, jams and jellies labeled as "sugar free." Sugar alcohols do provide some calories, but fewer calories than sugars. Sugar alcohols also occur naturally in fruits and vegetables. Examples of sugar alcohols are maltitol, mannitol, sorbitol, and xylitol. Compared to sugars, sugar alcohols are absorbed more slowly and are chemically broken down differently in the body. Look for sugar alcohols on the labels of sugarless gum and many sugar free and low carb sweets.

Because sugar alcohols are not completely absorbed, some (especially sorbitol and mannitol) may cause digestive discomfort for some people. The effects of sugar alcohols are related to the amount consumed, so read product labels and follow recommended serving size.

The Diabetes Food Pyramid

The Diabetes Food Pyramid is a handy way of remembering what foods you should eat every day. Based on the USDA Food Guide Pyramid, the Diabetes Food Pyramid has six main food groups and the recommended servings per day from each group. A healthy daily food plan for adults and adolescents includes servings from all the groups every day (except for Fats, Sweets & Alcohol Group).

Diabetes Pyramid Food Group	Servings Per Day
Grains, Beans & Starchy Vegetables	6 or more
Vegetables	3 to 5
Fruits	2 to 4
Milk & Milk Products	2 to 3
Meat & Meat Substitutes	2 to 3
Fats, Sweets & Alcohol	Small amounts

For more information, consult Exchange Lists for Meal Planning developed by the American Diabetes Association and the American Dietetic Association.

Food Exchanges

Food exchanges represent categories of foods grouped according to calories, fat, protein and carbohydrate content, and are derived from Exchange Lists for Meal Planning developed by the American Diabetes Association and the American Dietetic Association. A serving of a food in each group has about the same amount of carbohydrate, protein, fat and calories as other foods in the group.

Within a group, foods can be "exchanged" for one another. For example, 2 tablespoons of grated parmesan cheese and one ounce of lean pork are both equal to one lean meat exchange. Both foods have an average of 0 grams carbohydrate, 7 grams protein, 3 grams fat and 55 calories. In other words, 1 ounce of lean pork can be "exchanged" for 2 tablespoons parmesan cheese.

■ THE CARBOHYDRATE GROUP ■
The Carbohydrate Group includes the following food exchange lists:

Starch: (Cereal, grains, pasta, breads, peas, potatoes, cooked beans, peas, lentils)
One starch exchange equals 15 grams carbohydrate, 3 grams protein, 0 to 1 grams fat and 80 calories. Generally, one starch food exchange is:

½ cup cooked cereal	120 ml
⅓ cup cooked rice or pasta	80 ml
1 ounce bread product, such as 1 slice bread	28 g

Fruit: (Fruit, unsweetened fruit juice)
One fruit exchange equals 15 grams carbohydrate and 60 calories. One fruit exchange is:

1 small banana	
17 small grapes	
½ cup orange juice	120 ml

Milk: (Fat free, low fat, reduced fat, whole)
One milk exchange equals 12 grams carbohydrate and 8 grams protein. (Cheeses are on the Meat Food Exchange List and cream and other dairy fats are on the Fat Food Exchange List.) One milk food exchange is:

1 cup fat free milk (0 to 3 grams fat per serving)	240 ml
1 cup 2% milk (5 grams fat per serving)	240 ml
1 cup whole milk (8 grams fat per serving)	240 ml

Other Carbohydrates: (Sweets, desserts)
One other carbohydrate exchange equals 15 grams carbohydrate (or 1 starch or 1 fruit or 1 milk). One other carbohydrate exchange is:

1 (2 inch square) brownie, unfrosted (1 other carbohydrate, 1 fat)	5 cm
½ cup fat free no sugar added ice cream (1 other carbohydrate)	120 ml

Nonstarchy Vegetables: (Broccoli, tomatoes, salad greens)
One vegetable exchange (½ cooked or 1 cup/240 ml raw) equals 5 grams carbohydrate, 2 grams protein, 0 grams fat and 5 calories. One vegetable exchange is:

½ cup cooked mushrooms	120 ml
1 cup raw broccoli	240 ml

■ THE MEAT AND MEAT SUBSTITUTES GROUP ■

Meat and meat substitutes containing both protein and fat are in this group.
Generally, 1 meat exchange is:

1 ounce meat, poultry or cheese	28 g
½ cup beans, peas or lentils	120 ml

Categories within this group are named based on servings of the same amount of protein (7 grams), but differing amounts of fat and calories.

The Meat and Meat Substitutes Group includes the following categories:

Very Lean Meat and Substitutes: (0 grams carbohydrate, 7 grams protein, 0 to 1 grams fat, 35 calories) One ounce (28 g) chicken or turkey breast is 1 very lean meat exchange.

Lean Meat and Substitutes: (0 grams carbohydrate, 7 grams protein, 3 grams fat, 55 calories) One ounce (28 g) ground round is 1 lean meat exchange.

Medium Fat Meat and Substitutes: (0 grams carbohydrate, 7 grams protein, 5 grams fat, 75 calories) One egg is 1 medium fat meat exchange.

High Fat Meat and Substitutes: (0 grams carbohydrate, 7 grams protein, 8 grams fat, 100 calories) One ounce (28 g) pork sausage is 1 high fat meat exchange.

■ THE FAT GROUP ■

Based on the type of fat they contain, fats are divided into three groups: monounsaturated, polyunsaturated and saturated. In general, one fat exchange equals 5 grams fat and 45 calories:

1 teaspoon regular margarine	5 ml
1 teaspoon vegetable oil	5 ml
½ tablespoon peanut butter	7 ml
1 teaspoon regular mayonnaise	5 ml
1 tablespoon regular cream cheese	15 ml

■ FREE FOOD EXCHANGES ■

A free food is any food or drink that contains less than 20 calories or 5 grams or fewer carbohydrates per serving. Check serving sizes of free foods and limit to 3 servings per day. Free foods include:

Fat-free or reduced-fat foods (1 tablespoon (15 ml) fat-free or reduced-fat sour cream)

Sugar free foods (2 teaspoons (10 ml) no sugar added jelly)

Drinks (Coffee and sugar-free diet soft drinks)

Condiments (lemon juice, mustard, ¼ cup (60 ml) salsa)

Seasonings (Fresh or dried herbs, garlic, flavoring extracts)

Diabetes Terms

Diabetes mellitus: A chronic disorder characterized by high blood glucose (sugar) resulting from insufficient or ineffective insulin production in the body.

Type 1 diabetes: A less common type of diabetes in which the body produces no insulin at all (also known as insulin-dependent diabetes mellitus or juvenile-onset diabetes).

Recommendations for Type 1 diabetes: To maintain appropriate blood glucose levels requires commitment to a carefully planned program of diet, physical activity and insulin injections, as directed by their physician or dietitian.

Type 2 diabetes: A more common type of diabetes characterized by high blood glucose and insulin resistance (also known as noninsulin-dependent diabetes mellitus or adult-onset diabetes).

Recommendations for Type 2 diabetes: Persons with Type 2 diabetes benefit most from a diet that controls blood glucose fluctuations and promotes weight loss. To maintain appropriate blood glucose levels, the same amount of carbohydrate should be consumed every day. Eating too much or too little carbohydrate can lead to problems. People with Type 2 diabetes should daily monitor the amount of their carbohydrate intake, as directed by their physician or dietitian.

Source: Whitney, E.N., & Rolfes, S. R. Understanding Nutrition, 9th ed. Belmont, CA: Wadsworth/Thomson Learning, 2002 (p. 620-624).

■■■

8 Ways to Reduce Salt Intake

1. Remove the salt shaker from the table!
2. Always taste foods before adding salt.
3. Cook with reduced-sodium or salt-free seasoning blends.
4. Use salt substitutes, such as those made with potassium chloride.
5. Use sodium-free herbs such as parsley, mint, basil, thyme, oregano and rosemary or herb blends.
6. Use sodium-free spices such as curry, ginger and pepper.
7. Use flavorings such as lemon juice, vinegar and wine.
8. Look for these product labels:
   Sodium-free, salt-free: less than 5 mg sodium per serving.
   Low-sodium: 140 mg or less per serving.
   Very low sodium: 35 mg or less per serving.

Sodium Q & A

Why do we like salt?

Salt gives food its own tangy taste, enhances other flavors and even suppresses bitter flavors. Throughout history, salt has been highly regarded. It simply tastes good!

How much sodium do I need?

Sodium is critical to bodily functions such as maintenance of balance of fluids, nerve transmissions and muscle contractions in the body.

Foods actually provide more sodium than the body needs. Our diets are rarely low in sodium. The minimum sodium requirement for adults is set at 500 milligrams in the United States. The maximum sodium requirement for adults is set at 2400 milligrams or 6 grams of sodium per day.

Which foods are low in sodium?

In general, unprocessed foods such as fresh fruits and vegetables have the least sodium. Milk and meats have moderate amounts of sodium.

Which foods should I avoid?

Processed foods generally have the most sodium. Researchers report that as much as 75% of the sodium in our diets comes from salt added to foods by manufacturers. About 15% comes from salt added during cooking and at the table. About 10% comes from the natural content in foods.

Use these products sparingly:

Salty snacks such as potato chips, pretzels, salted popcorn, salted nuts and crackers
Salty or smoked meats such as bacon, frankfurters, sausage, lunch meats and ham
Foods prepared in brine, such as pickles, olives and sauerkraut
Salty condiments such as seasoned salts, MSG, bouillon cubes, ketchup and mustard
Sauces such as soy, teriyaki, worcestershire and barbecue
Cheeses, especially processed cheeses
Canned and instant soups

Cooking For Success

Read through the entire recipe:

Check nutritional analysis and food exchanges
Note preparation time required
Check ingredients list for specific preparation required (crushed, diced, sliced)
Check for use of water, salt substitute, pepper, and non-stick cooking spray ("free" ingredients)
Note optional ingredients or recipe variations
Note tools and cooking utensils (such as measuring spoons/cups, meat thermometer, non-stick skillet, wire mesh strainer, wire whisk)
Check procedures and order (such as preheating oven)

Assemble ingredients, tools and utensils needed:

Measure and/or prepare ingredients as directed
Check to see if you need a timer
Check to see if you need plastic wrap, aluminum foil, etc.
Check to see if you have the size of baking and/or serving dish required or can substitute

Prepare the recipe:

Follow recipe directions in order given
Follow times and temperatures for cooking
Follow methods for how food should be handled (mix, stir, toss)
Check descriptions of how to tell doneness of a food
Check to see if food should be served immediately or should be chilled before serving
Note suggested ways of serving (dessert plates or bowls, stemmed glasses)
Follow directions for serving sizes

Good News About Splenda®

According to recent research, sucralose (found in Splenda®), like sugar alcohols, does not elevate blood sugar levels in the body. Findings were that sucralose and sugar alcohols do NOT contribute to the overall or "net" amount of carbohydrates in a serving of food.

~Dr. Sally Hunt

Appetizers & Beverages

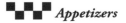

Rolled Enchilada Bites

Net Carbs: 4 g

1 (1 pound) package ground turkey breast or extra-lean ground beef	.5 kg
1 (10 ounce) can mild red chili enchilada sauce or Red Chili Enchilada Sauce, (p. 146)	280 g
8 (10 inch) low-carb whole wheat tortillas	25 cm
2½ cups shredded reduced-fat cheddar or jack cheese	600 ml

1. In sprayed heavy skillet over medium heat, cook and stir meat about 8 to 10 minutes. Remove meat from skillet. (If using beef, drain in wire mesh strainer and rinse to remove fat. Wipe skillet with paper towels.)

2. Preheat oven to 375° (190° C).

3. Return meat to skillet, add enchilada sauce and simmer 10 minutes over medium heat. Season to taste with salt substitute and pepper.

4. Spray both sides of each tortilla with cooking spray. Spread each tortilla with 2 tablespoons (30 ml) meat and 1 tablespoon (15 ml) cheese. Roll tightly.

5. On sprayed baking sheet, arrange rolled enchiladas seam side down. Spray enchiladas again with cooking spray.

6. Bake at 375° (190° C) 10 to 15 minutes or until cheese melts. Cut each rolled enchilada into quarters and serve immediately.

Yield: 32 servings (32 enchilada quarters)   Serving size: 1   quarter

Calories: 115	Protein: 10 g	Carbohydrate: 4 g
Fat: 7 g	Cholesterol: 25 mg	Sodium: 335 mg
Calcium: 255 mg	Fiber: less than 1 g	Sugars: 0 g
Sugar Alcohol: 0 g		

Food Exchanges: 1 medium fat meat, ½ bread

■ ■ ■

❧ Hot Asparagus Roll-Ups

Net Carbs: 11 g

10 fresh asparagus spears, trimmed

10 slices sugar-free wheat bread, crusts trimmed

1½ tablespoons light mayonnaise   **22 ml**

**5 reduced-fat mozzarella or cheddar string cheese sticks,
    pulled apart**

1. In wide skillet, heat 1 inch (2.5 cm) water until it boils. Add asparagus, cover and cook 7 to 10 minutes. Do not overcook. Drain well and set aside.

2. With rolling pin, slightly flatten each trimmed bread slice. Spread about 1 teaspoon (5 ml) mayonnaise on one side of bread.

3. Top each bread slice with 1 or 2 asparagus spears and 3 to 4 cheese strings. Roll up carefully.

4. On sprayed baking sheet, arrange rolls seam side down and coat with cooking spray.

5. Broil 3 to 5 minutes about 5 inches below heat until bread toasts.

6. Serve immediately.

Yield: 10 servings   Serving size: 1 roll

Calories: 110   Protein: 7 g   Carbohydrate: 14 g
Fat: 3 g   Cholesterol: 6 mg   Sodium: 218 mg
Calcium: 86 mg   Fiber: 3 g   Sugars: 1 g
Sugar Alcohol: 0 g

Food Exchanges: 1½ bread, 1 vegetable, ½ fat

■ ■ ■

Zucchini Smiles

Net Carbs: 3 g

2 zucchini, sliced in ¾-inch (1.8 cm) thick slices

2 tablespoons bite-size crispy corn cereal squares,
crushed   **30 ml**

1 tablespoon grated parmesan or romano cheese   **15 ml**

3 tablespoons light mayonnaise   **45 ml**

1. In medium saucepan, heat ½ inch (1.8 cm) water until it boils. Add zucchini slices, reduce heat to simmer and cover.

2. Cook 3 to 5 minutes, just until zucchini becomes tender. Drain and cool on paper towels.

3. Mix crushed cereal and cheese. Spread mayonnaise evenly on one side of each zucchini slice. Coat that side with cheese mixture and spray lightly with cooking spray.

4. On sprayed baking sheet, broil zucchini slices 4 to 5 inches (13 - 15 cm) below heat source about 4 to 6 minutes.

5. Serve hot.

Yield: 7 servings (about 14 to 16 slices)   Serving size: 2 slices

Calories: 35	Protein: less than 1 g	Carbohydrate: 3 g
Fat: 2 g	Cholesterol: 3 mg	Sodium: 60 mg
Calcium: 18 mg	Fiber: less than 1 g	Sugars: 1 g
Sugar Alcohol: 0 g		

Food Exchanges: ½ fat

■ ■ ■

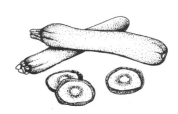

Easy Porcupine Meatballs

Net Carbs: 16 g

1 (1 pound) package ground turkey or lean ground beef (or mixture of turkey and beef)	.5 kg
1 (10 ounce) can Campbell's® Healthy Request® cream of mushroom condensed soup	280 g
1 cup uncooked converted or parboiled long grain rice	240 ml
⅓ cup chopped green onion	80 ml

1. Preheat oven to 350° (176° C).

2. Combine all ingredients and mix well. Season to taste with salt substitute and pepper.

3. Form meat mixture into balls of about 2 tablespoons (30 ml) each. (For easier handling, spray hands with non-stick cooking spray and scoop and pack mixture into ice cream scoop.)

4. In sprayed 8-inch (20 cm) square baking dish, arrange meatballs. Cover and bake 1 hour or until rice is tender. (Parboiled or converted rice cooks in about 25 minutes.)

5. Uncover and bake 10 minutes or until meatballs brown. Drain on paper towels, then serve or freeze for later use.

Optional: Serve with no-salt tomato sauce, Carb Options™ garden-style pasta sauce or Carb Options™ alfredo sauce.

Yield: 10 to 12 servings   Serving size: 1 meatball

Calories: 140   Protein: 9 g   Carbohydrate: 16 g
Fat: 4 g   Cholesterol: 34 mg   Sodium: 126 mg
Calcium: 40 mg   Fiber: less than 1 g   Sugars: less than 1 g
Sugar Alcohol: 0 g

Food Exchanges: 1 bread, 1 other carb, ½ medium fat meat

■ ■ ■

Saucy Chicken Wings

Net Carbs: less than 1 g

20 frozen chicken wing sections, thawed

Salt-free Creole seasoning to taste

Garlic powder to taste

½ to 1 cup Carb Options™ barbecue sauce　　　　　**120-240 ml**

1. Preheat oven to 325° (162° C).

2. On sprayed foil-lined baking sheet, arrange chicken wings. Sprinkle with seasonings and pepper to taste.

3. Brush wings with barbecue sauce and bake at 325° (162°) for about 30 minutes.

4. Turn wings over and brush other sides with sauce. Return to oven and bake 30 more minutes or until chicken is fork-tender and crisp.

Yield: 10 servings　　　　　Serving size: 2 pieces

Calories: 62　　　　　　　Protein: 5 g　　　　　　　Carbohydrate: less than 1 g
Fat: 5 g　　　　　　　　　Cholesterol: 24 mg　　　　Sodium: 153 mg
Calcium: 0 mg　　　　　　Fiber: 0 g　　　　　　　　Sugars: 0 g
Sugar Alcohol: 0 g
Food Exchanges: ½ medium fat meat

■ ■ ■

Veggie Nachos

Net Carbs: 3 g

4 cups cut vegetables	**1 kg**
1½ cups finely shredded reduced-fat	
cheddar or jack cheese	**360 ml**
2 to 3 tablespoons canned mild diced green chilies,	
drained	**30-45 ml**
2 to 3 tablespoons sliced ripe olives, drained	**30-45 ml**

1. Preheat broiler. On ovenproof serving platter, arrange vegetable pieces (celery and carrot sticks, squash slices, bell pepper strips, cauliflower and broccoli florets) and sprinkle with cheese, chilies and olives.

2. Broil 4 to 6 inches (10-15 cm) from heat about 5 to 7 minutes or until cheese melts. Serve immediately.

Yield: 6 to 8 servings   Serving size: ½ cup (120 ml)

Calories: 180	Protein: 13 g	Carbohydrate: 5 g
Fat: 13 g	Cholesterol: 35 mg	Sodium: 419 mg
Calcium: 380 mg	Fiber: 2 g	Sugars: 3 g
Sugar Alcohol: 0 g		

Food Exchanges: 1½ fat, ½ medium fat meat, ½ vegetable

Party Cheese Squares

Net Carbs: 1 g

4 cups shredded reduced-fat cheddar cheese	**.9 L**
1 cup Egg Beaters® egg substitute	**240 ml**
1 (4 ounce) can mild diced green chilies, drained	**114 g**
⅓ cup finely chopped green onions with tops	**80 ml**

1. Preheat oven to 325° (162˚ C). Mix all ingredients and spread into sprayed 8 x 8-inch (20 x 20 cm) square baking dish. Bake 30 minutes or until table knife inserted in middle comes out clean. Cut into 1½-inch (3.5 cm) squares and serve hot.

Yield: 25 servings (about 25 squares)   Serving size: 1 square

Calories: 128	Protein: 10 g	Carbohydrate: 2 g
Fat: 9 g	Cholesterol: 26 mg	Sodium: 419 mg
Calcium: 315 mg	Fiber: 1 g	Sugars: less than 1 g
Sugar Alcohol: 0 g		

Food Exchanges: 0

❧ Neptune's Favorite Shrimp Dip

Net Carbs: 1 g

This delicious dip disappears quickly!

1 (8 ounce) package reduced-fat cream cheese (Neufchatel)	**227 g**
½ cup light mayonnaise	**120 ml**
1 (6 ounce) can peeled-veined shrimp, drained, rinsed, chopped or 1 cup frozen peeled-veined shrimp, /slightly thawed	**168 g**
1½ teaspoons salt-free Creole seasoning	**7 ml**

1. To soften cheese for mixing, remove foil wrapper and place in small microwave-safe bowl. Heat on HIGH power about 5 seconds.

2. Stir in mayonnaise.

3. Add shrimp and seasoning blend and mix well.

4. Chill 1 hour before serving.

Yield: 18 servings (About 2¼ cups/540 ml)

Serving size: 2 tablespoons (30 ml)

Calories: 66
Fat: 5 g
Calcium: 15 mg
Sugar Alcohol: 0 g

Protein: 3 g
Cholesterol: 28 mg
Fiber: 0 g

Carbohydrate: 1 g
Sodium: 106 mg
Sugars: less than 1 g

Food Exchanges: ½ fat

■ ■ ■

❧ Hot Artichoke Appetizer

Net Carbs: 3 g

2 (8½ ounce) cans artichoke hearts in water, drained, chopped	2 (237 g)
1 (4 ounce) can mild diced green chilies, drained	114 g
6 tablespoons light mayonnaise	90 ml
1½ cups finely shredded reduced-fat cheddar cheese	360 ml

1. Preheat oven to 350° (176° C). In sprayed 11 x 7-inch (28 x 18 cm) baking dish, spread chopped artichokes and top with chilies. Carefully spread mayonnaise over chilies and sprinkle with cheese. Cover and bake 15 minutes or until mixture bubbles and heats through. Serve immediately.

Yield: 20 servings (About 2½ cups/560 ml)   Serving size: 2 tablespoons (30 ml)

Calories: 79	Protein: 5 g	Carbohydrate: 3 g
Fat: 6 g	Cholesterol: 14 mg	Sodium: 232 mg
Calcium: 126 mg	Fiber: less than 1 g	Sugars: less than 1 g
Sugar Alcohol: 0 g		

Food Exchanges: ½ fat

Dippy Spinach Special

Net Carbs: 2 g

1 (10 ounce) package frozen chopped spinach, thawed	280 g
⅓ cup green onions with tops, finely chopped	80 g
1 tablespoon fresh lemon juice	15 ml
1 (8 ounce) carton light sour cream	227 g

1. In wire mesh strainer, drain spinach and squeeze out as much liquid as possible. In food processor or blender, process all ingredients until smooth. Season to taste with salt substitute and pepper. Cover and chill at least 2 hours before serving.

Yield: 16 servings (About 2 cups/480 ml)   Serving size: 2 tablespoons (30 ml)

Calories: 23	Protein: 1 g	Carbohydrate: 2 g
Fat: 1 g	Cholesterol: 5 mg	Sodium: 34 mg
Calcium: 42 mg	Fiber: less than 1 g	Sugars: 1 g
Sugar Alcohol: 0 g		

Food Exchanges: 0

Pita Crisps

Net Carbs: 8 g

4 whole wheat pita breads

1. Preheat oven to 350° (176° C). With sharp knife, cut each pita bread to make 12 single wedges. Spray wedges lightly with cooking spray. Place wedges on baking sheet.

2. Bake 8 to 10 minutes or until wedges are light brown and crisp. Serve immediately or store in airtight container. Optional: Before baking, sprinkle wedges with herb or spice of your choice.

Yield: 16 servings (48 wedges)   Serving size: 3 wedges

Calories: 43   Protein: 2 g   Carbohydrate: 9 g
Fat: less than 1 g   Cholesterol: 0 mg   Sodium: 85 mg
Calcium: 2 mg   Fiber: 1 g   Sugars: less than 1 g
Sugar Alcohol: 0 g
Food Exchanges: ½ bread

■ ■ ■

❧ No-Guilt Tortilla Crisps

Net Carbs: 4 g

12 (8 inch) low-carb whole wheat tortillas   12 (20 cm)
Non-stick cooking spray

1. Preheat oven to 325° (162° C). In batches, stack and cut tortillas into 6 wedges. Place on wax paper or parchment paper and spray with non-stick cooking spray on both sides.

2. On sprayed baking sheet, bake wedges at 325° (162° C) for 20 to 30 minutes or until they brown and become crisp. Cool and store in airtight container.

Yield: 12 servings (72 wedges)   Serving size: 4 to 6 wedges

Calories: 70   Protein: 4 g   Carbohydrate: 7 g
Fat: 4 g   Cholesterol: 0 mg   Sodium: 250 mg
Calcium: 0 mg   Fiber: 3 g   Sugars: 0 g
Sugar Alcohol: 0 g
Food Exchanges: 1 fat, ½ bread

Wakka-Moley

Net Carbs: 2 g

2 ripe avocados	
1 teaspoon grated onion	**5 ml**
2 teaspoons fresh lime juice	**10 ml**
¼ teaspoon garlic salt or powder	**1 ml**

1. Halve avocados and remove seeds. Cut halves into quarters and peel. Mash avocado with fork.

2. Combine all ingredients. If using garlic powder, season to taste with salt substitute. Cover tightly until ready to serve. Optional: Serve with No-Guilt Tortilla Crisps (p. 24)

Yield: 4 servings (about 1 cup/240 ml)
Calories: 143
Fat: 13 g
Calcium: 11 mg
Sugar Alcohol: 0 g
Food Exchanges: 2½ fat, 1 vegetable

Protein: 2 g
Cholesterol: 0 mg
Fiber: 6 g

Serving size: ¼ cup (60 ml)
Carbohydrate: 8 g
Sodium: 67 mg
Sugars: less than 1 g

❧ Sesame-Cheddar Balls

Net Carbs: 1 g

1 (8 ounce) package reduced-fat cream cheese (Neufchatel)	**227 g**
2 (8 ounce) packages finely shredded reduced-fat cheddar cheese	**227 g**
2 tablespoons finely chopped green onions with tops	**30 ml**
3 tablespoons sesame seeds	**45 ml**

1. In mixing bowl, mix cream cheese, cheddar cheese and green onions. Cover and chill at least 4 hours.

2. In dry skillet over medium heat, stir and toast sesame seeds until seeds are golden brown and fragrant. Remove from heat and cool. Form cheese mixture into 1-inch (2.5 cm) balls and roll in toasted sesame seeds. Chill before serving.

Yield: 12 servings (about 2½ cups/600ml)
Calories: 178
Fat: 14 g
Calcium: 301 mg
Sugar Alcohol: 0 g
Food Exchanges: 1 fat, ½ medium fat meat

Protein: 12 g
Cholesterol: 40 mg
Fiber: less than 1 g

Serving size: 2 balls
Carbohydrate: 1 g
Sodium: 350 mg
Sugars: less than 1 g

Perfect Deviled Eggs

Net Carbs: less than 1 g

Everybody's favorite!

6 eggs
3 tablespoons light or fat-free mayonnaise   **45 ml**
2 teaspoons dijon-style or yellow mustard   **10 ml**
⅛ to ¼ teaspoon salt-free Creole or other seasoning,
    divided   **.5 - 1 ml**

1. To prevent cracking, set eggs at room temperature 10 to 15 minutes before cooking.

2. In large saucepan, heat 4 inches water until it boils. With large spoon, carefully lower each egg into boiling water.

3. Maintain medium boil and continue to cook eggs for 10 minutes. Remove eggs and plunge into cold or ice water.

4. Carefully crack shells all around eggs. Remove shells from eggs and slice eggs in half lengthwise.

5. With fork, carefully remove and thoroughly mash egg yolks. Add mayonnaise, mustard and seasoning to yolks. Beat together with fork until mixture is creamy and smooth.

6. Mound egg yolk mixture evenly into cooked egg whites, covering egg yolk holes. Sprinkle each yolk with dash seasoning.

7. Cover and chill before serving.

Optional: Substitute 2 to 3 dashes hot sauce and salt substitute to taste for Creole seasoning blend.

Yield: 12 servings   Serving size: 1 deviled egg half

Calories: 52   Protein: 3 g   Carbohydrate: less than 1 g
Fat: 4 g   Cholesterol: 107 mg   Sodium: 74 mg
Calcium: 14 mg   Fiber: 0 g   Sugars: less than 1 g
Sugar Alcohol: 0 g

Food Exchanges: ½ medium fat meat

■ ■ ■

Snappy Chicken Spread

Net Carbs: 2 g

1 cup chopped cooked chicken breast	**240 ml**
¼ to ⅓ cup light mayonnaise	**60 - 80 ml**
½ cup sliced celery	**120 ml**
¼ cup diced pimento with liquid	**60 ml**

1. In food processor or blender, combine all ingredients until they mix well.

2. Season to taste with salt substitute and pepper.

Yield: 6 servings (about 1½ cups/360 ml)　　　　Serving size: ¼ cup (60 ml)

Calories: 58　　　　Protein: 7 g　　　　Carbohydrate: 2 g
Fat: 2 g　　　　Cholesterol: 20 mg　　　　Sodium: 110 mg
Calcium: 7 mg　　　　Fiber: less than 1 g　　　　Sugars: less than 1 g
Sugar Alcohol: 0 g

Food Exchanges: ½ lean meat

■ ■ ■

Jezebel's Cream Cheese Spread

Net Carbs: 4 g

½ cup low-sugar apricot fruit spread	**120 ml**
1 to 2 tablespoons prepared horseradish	**15-30 ml**
1 (8 ounce) package reduced fat cream cheese (Neufchatel)	**227 g**

1. Mix fruit spread, horseradish and ¼ teaspoon (1 ml) ground black pepper.

2. Spoon over block of cream cheese.

Yield: 16 servings (about 2 cups/480 ml) cheese with sauce　　　　Serving size: 2 tablespoons (30 ml)

Calories: 49　　　　Protein: 2 g　　　　Carbohydrate: 4 g
Fat: 3 g　　　　Cholesterol: 10 mg　　　　Sodium: 63 mg
Calcium: 11 mg　　　　Fiber: less than 1 g　　　　Sugars: 3 g
Sugar Alcohol: 0 g

Food Exchanges: ½ fat

California-Dreamin' Tuna Spread

Net Carbs: 1 g

2 large avocados, pitted, peeled, slightly mashed	
1 (6 ounce) can solid white albacore tuna in water, drained	**168 g**
2 tablespoons fresh lemon juice	**30 ml**
2 teaspoons prepared horseradish	**10 ml**

1. Combine all ingredients and mix well. Cover tightly and chill before serving. Optional: Add dash bottled hot pepper sauce or salt-free Creole seasoning.

Yield: 8 servings (2 cups/480 ml)   Serving size: ¼ cup (60 ml)

Calories: 100   Protein: 7 g   Carbohydrate: 4 g
Fat: 7 g   Cholesterol: 10 g   Sodium: 101 mg
Calcium: 8 mg   Fiber: 3 g   Sugars: less than 1 g
Sugar Alcohol: 0 g

Food Exchanges: 1 medium fat meat, ½ fat

■ ■ ■

Chickpea Hummus

Net Carbs: 14 g

2 cloves garlic, minced	
1 (15 ounce) can chickpeas (garbanzo beans), drained, rinsed	**425 g**
1 tablespoon sesame seeds, toasted	**15 ml**
2 to 2½ tablespoons fresh lemon juice	**30 - 37 ml**

1. In sprayed skillet over medium heat, cook and stir garlic 1 to 2 minutes. In food processor, blend all ingredients until smooth. Season to taste with salt substitute and pepper. Chill 1 to 2 hours for flavors to blend.

Tip: Use 2 to 3 tablespoons (30 - 45 ml) tahini (sesame seed paste) instead of sesame seeds if you prefer. Optional: Serve with Pita Crisps (p. 24)

Yield: 6 servings (about 1½ cups/360 ml)   Serving size: ¼ cup (60 ml)
Calories: 96   Protein: 4 g   Carbohydrate: 17 g
Fat: 2 g   Cholesterol: 0 mg   Sodium: 212 mg
Calcium: 40 mg   Fiber: 3 g   Sugars: 4 g
Sugar Alcohol: 0 g
Food Exchanges: 1 bread, ½ fat

Frosty Strawberry Soda

Net Carbs: 14 g

1½ cups skim milk	**360 ml**
1½ cups sliced fresh strawberries	**360 ml**
2 cups no-sugar-added strawberry ice cream	**480 ml**
1 (16 ounce) bottle club soda	**.5 kg**

1. In blender, process milk and strawberries 10 to 15 seconds. Pour into 5 tall glasses.

2. Add small scoop strawberry ice cream to each glass. Slowly add soda to fill about ½ inch (1.2 cm) from top of glass.

3. Serve immediately with straw and iced teaspoon.

Tip: If you like, use 1 (10 ounce/280 ml) package unsweetened sliced strawberries, partially thawed, instead of fresh strawberries.

Optional: Garnish with fresh strawberry.

Variation: To reduce net carbs, substitute low-carb ice cream.

Yield: 6 servings   Serving size: About 1 cup (240 ml)

Calories: 92	Protein: 4 g	Carbohydrate: 14 g
Fat: 2 g	Cholesterol: 8 mg	Sodium: 77 mg
Calcium: 101 mg	Fiber: less than 1 g	Sugars: 7 g
Sugar Alcohol: 0 g		

Food Exchanges: ½ milk, ½ fruit

◆

*Whole fruit is more filling than fruit juice
and generally has more fiber.*

Raspberry-Pineapple Freeze

Net Carbs: 19 g

The ice cubes turn into pink punch as they melt!

1 (.3 ounce) packet sugar-free raspberry soft drink mix	**12 g**
½ cup Splenda® sugar substitute	**120 ml**
4 cups unsweetened pineapple juice	**.9 L**
2 to 3 (12 ounce) cans diet lemon-lime soda, chilled	**2-3 (340 g)**

1. In large bowl, mix soft drink powder, sugar substitute and juice. Pour into 2 ice cube trays and freeze.

2. To serve, place cubes in glasses and fill with diet soda.

Yield: 8 servings (24 cubes)   Serving size: 3 cubes

Calories: 75	Protein: less than 1 g	Carbohydrate: 19 g
Fat: less than 1 g	Cholesterol: 0 mg	Sodium: 12 mg
Calcium: 21 mg	Fiber: less than 1 g	Sugars: 17 g
Sugar Alcohol: 0 g		

Food Exchanges: 1 fruit

■ ■ ■

Skinny Black Cow

Net Carbs: 19 g

1 (12 ounce) can diet root beer, chilled	**340 g**
½ cup no-sugar-added vanilla ice cream	**120 ml**

1. Into tall 10-ounce (280 g) glass, pour diet root beer. Top with ice cream.

2. Serve immediately with straw and iced teaspoon.

Variation: To reduce net carbs, substitute low-carb ice cream.

Yield: 1 serving   Serving size: 1½ cups (360 ml)

Calories: 91	Protein: 3 g	Carbohydrate: 19 g
Fat: 0 g	Cholesterol: 0 mg	Sodium: 122 mg
Calcium: 80 mg	Fiber: 0 g	Sugars: 4 g
Sugar Alcohol: 0 g		

Food Exchanges: 0

Old-Time Lemonade

Net Carbs: 8 g

1 cup Splenda® sugar substitute
1 cup fresh lemon juice
Lemon slices for garnish
Mint sprigs for garnish

240 ml
240 ml

1. In large pitcher, combine sugar substitute, lemon juice and 1 cup (240 ml) water and stir until sugar substitute dissolves. Add 4 cups (.9 L) water. Serve over ice with lemon slices and mint sprigs.

Yield: 6 servings (about 6½ cups/1.6 L)   Serving size: 1 cup (240 ml)

Calories: 10   Protein: less than 1 g   Carbohydrate: 8 g
Fat: 0 g   Cholesterol: 0 mg   Sodium: less than 1 mg
Calcium: 3 mg   Fiber: less than 1 g   Sugars: less than 1 g
Sugar Alcohol: 0 g

Food Exchanges: 0

■■■

Lemon-Lime Punch Smoothie

Net Carbs: 8 g

1 (.3 ounce) packet sugar-free lemon-lime
    soft drink mix   12 g
4 cups skim milk   .9 L
2 cups no-sugar-added vanilla ice cream
    or frozen yogurt   480 ml
1 to 2 (12 ounce) cans diet lemon-lime soda   1 -2 (340 g)

1. In large punch bowl, combine soft drink mix with milk and stir until it dissolves. Add ice cream or yogurt in small spoonfuls.

2. Carefully pour soda down side of punch bowl. Stir gently with vertical motion. Serve immediately.

Yield: 15 servings (about 7½ cups/1.9 L)   Serving size: ½ cup (120 ml)
Calories: 48   Protein: 3 g   Carbohydrate: 8 g
Fat: less than 1 g   Cholesterol: 1 mg   Sodium: 44 mg
Calcium: 81 mg   Fiber: 0 g   Sugars: 4 g
Sugar Alcohol: 0 g
Food Exchanges: ½ milk

Fruit Tea Fizz

Net Carbs: 5 g

Make this really fast with the new cold brew tea bags!

5 to 6 (regular size) or 2 to 3 (family size) decaffeinated tea bags	
½ cup Splenda® sugar substitute	**120 ml**
1 cup fresh orange juice	**240 ml**
1½ (12 ounce) cans diet lemon-lime soda or 2 to 3 cups club soda	**1½ (340 g); 480-710 ml**

1. In large saucepan, pour 3 cups (710 ml) boiling water over tea bags. Cover and let stand 5 minutes. Remove tea bags. Add sugar substitute and stir until it dissolves.

2. Add orange juice and pour into pitcher with 2 cups (480 ml) ice cubes.

3. Just before serving, carefully pour soda down side of pitcher.

Variation: *Substitute ½ cup (120 ml) orange juice and ⅓ cup (80 ml) fresh lemon juice for 1 cup (240 ml) orange juice. Substitute 1 cup (240 ml) reduced-calorie cranberry juice cocktail for 1 cup (240 ml) orange juice.*

Yield: 8 servings (8 cups/1.9 L) Serving size: 1 cup (240 ml)

Calories: 15	Protein: less than 1 g	Carbohydrate: 5 g
Fat: less than 1 g	Cholesterol: 0 mg	Sodium: 10 mg
Calcium: 3 mg	Fiber: less than 1 g	Sugars: 0 g
Sugar Alcohol: 0 g	Food Exchanges: 0	

■ ■ ■

Sugar-Free Hot Cocoa

Net Carbs: 11 g

4 tablespoons unsweetened cocoa	**60 ml**
2 tablespoons Splenda® sugar substitute	**30 ml**
3¼ cups skim milk	**770 ml**
½ teaspoon vanilla	**2 ml**

1. In medium heavy saucepan, mix cocoa and sugar substitute. Over medium heat, add ½ cup (120 ml) milk, stirring constantly with wire whisk until dry ingredients dissolve.

2. Gradually add remaining milk and cook and stir just until cocoa bubbles. Remove from heat and stir in vanilla. Serve immediately.

Optional: Top with ground cinnamon or nutmeg.

Yield: 4 servings   Serving size: ¾ cup (180 ml)
Calories: 79   Protein: 8 g   Carbohydrate: 13 g
Fat: less than 1 g   Cholesterol: 4 mg   Sodium: 89 mg
Calcium: 188 mg   Fiber: 2 g   Sugars: 10 g
Sugar Alcohol: 0 g   Food Exchanges: ½ milk, ½ other carb

■ ■ ■

Hot Cranberry Tea

Net Carbs: 11 g

Clove-Cinnamon Spice Mix (p. 34)

⅓ cup Splenda® sugar substitute	**80 ml**
1 cup reduced-calorie cranberry juice cocktail	**240 ml**
4 (regular size) decaffeinated tea bags	

1. In saucepan, heat 1 cup (240 ml) water until it boils and add Clove-Cinnamon Spice Mix. Reduce heat, cover and simmer 10 minutes. Add 1 cup (240 ml) water, sugar substitute and cranberry juice and heat to boiling again.

2. Remove from heat, add tea bags and cover. Let stand 5 minutes. Remove tea bags and spice mix and serve.

Yield: 3 servings (about 3 cups/710 ml)   Serving size: 1 cup (240 ml)
Calories: 56   Protein: less than 1 g   Carbohydrate: 14 g
Fat: 2 g   Cholesterol: 0 mg   Sodium: 49 mg
Calcium: 80 mg   Fiber: 3 g   Sugars: 4 g
Sugar Alcohol: 0 g   Food Exchanges: 1 fruit

Hot Spicy Orange Tea

Net Carbs: 13 g

Clove-Cinnamon Spice Mix (below)
⅓ cup Splenda® sugar substitute   **80 ml**
1 cup fresh orange juice   **240 ml**
4 (regular size) decaffeinated tea bags

1. In saucepan, heat 1 cup (240 ml) water until it boils and add Clove-Cinnamon Spice Mix.

2. Reduce heat, cover and simmer 10 minutes. Add 1 cup (240 ml) water, sugar substitute and orange juice and heat to boiling again.

3. Remove from heat, add tea bags and cover. Let stand 5 minutes. Remove tea bags and spice mix and serve.

Yield: 3 servings   Serving size: 1 cup (240 ml)

Calories: 48   Protein: less than 1 g   Carbohydrate: 13 g
Fat: less than 1 g   Cholesterol: 0 mg   Sodium: 12 mg
Calcium: 27 mg   Fiber: less than 1 g   Sugars: less than 1 g
Sugar Alcohol: 0 g

Food Exchanges: 1 fruit

Clove-Cinnamon Spice Mix

10 whole cloves
1 cinnamon stick, broken
Metal tea holder, ball or cheesecloth square

Place cloves and cinnamon in metal tea holder or ball or tie in cheesecloth square.

Yield: Mix for 2 cups tea (480 ml)

■ ■ ■

Breakfast
& Brunch

Breakfast-Yogurt Parfait

Net Carbs: 21 g

½ cup fresh blueberries	120 ml
½ cup sliced fresh strawberries	120 ml
1 (6 ounce) carton low-carb strawberry yogurt, divided	168 g
¼ cup high-fiber, high-protein granola cereal	60 ml

1. Combine blueberries and strawberries and place ¼ cup (60 ml) fruit mixture in each of 2 tall parfait glass. Top fruit with 3 tablespoons (45 ml) yogurt and half the cereal.

2. Add remaining fruit, reserve a few pieces for garnish. Top with remaining yogurt and garnish with reserved fruit.

Tip: If you do not have fresh fruit, try ½ cup (120 ml) frozen blueberries, slightly thawed, and ½ cup (120 ml) frozen sliced strawberries, slightly thawed.

Yield: 2 servings
Calories: 191
Fat: 3 g
Calcium: 33 mg
Sugar Alcohol: 0 g

Serving size: 1 parfait
Protein: 10 g
Cholesterol: 8 mg
Fiber: 7 g
Food Exchanges: 1 bread, ½ fruit, ½ milk, ½ fat

Carbohydrate: 28 g
Sodium: 145 mg
Sugars: 14 g

■ ■ ■

Cantaloupe Fruit Bowl

Net Carbs: 34 g

2 small cantaloupes	
1 cup honeydew melon balls	240 ml
1 cup canned pineapple tidbits in juice, drained, chilled	240 ml
1 cup fresh blueberries	240 ml

1. Halve cantaloupes stem end to stem end and remove seeds with spoon. With melon baller, scoop balls from inside cantaloupe.

2. Arrange cantaloupe balls, honeydew balls, and drained pineapple tidbits in cantaloupe halves. Sprinkle tops with blueberries. Cover and chill. Serve within 1 to 2 hours for best results.

Yield: 4 servings
Calories: 151
Fat: less than 1 g
Calcium: 27 mg
Sugar Alcohol: 0 g

Serving size: ½ cantaloupe with fruit
Protein: 3 g
Cholesterol: 0 mg
Dietary Fiber: 4 g
Food Exchanges: 2½ fruit

Carbohydrate: 38 g
Sodium: 54 mg
Sugars: 33 g

Good Morning Grapefruit

Net Carbs: 11 g

2 large grapefruit, halved	
2 tablespoons Smart Balance® buttery spread	**30 ml**
Few drops orange extract or ½ teaspoon cinnamon	**2 ml**
2 teaspoons Splenda® sugar substitute	**10 ml**

1. With grapefruit knife or paring knife, section each grapefruit half by cutting around each section close to membrane. Sections should be loosened from shell completely.

2. In small saucepan, melt buttery spread or melt in microwave. Add orange extract and sugar substitute and mix well. Drizzle over grapefruit halves.

3. In shallow baking pan about 4 inches (10 cm) from heat, broil grapefruit halves until tops bubble and turn light brown.

Tip: If you can find pink grapefruit, they are usually sweeter.

Yield: 4 servings

Serving size: 1 grapefruit half

Calories: 92
Fat: 5 g
Calcium: 27 mg
Sugar Alcohol: 0 g

Protein: less than 1 g
Cholesterol: 0 mg
Fiber: 2 g
Food Exchanges: 1 fat, ½ fruit, ½ other carb

Carbohydrate: 13 g
Sodium: 45 mg
Sugars: 8 g

■ ■ ■

⅔ Fancy Seafood Grits

Net Carbs: 26 g

1 cup quick-cooking grits	240 ml
¼ cup chopped green onions with tops	60 ml
1 pound fresh or 1 (16 ounce) package frozen shrimp, peeled, veined	.5 kg
Grated parmesan cheese with basil, garlic and parsley	

1. Cook grits according to package instructions for 4 servings. Set aside and keep warm.

2. In sprayed non-stick skillet over medium heat, cook and stir green onions about 1 minute. Add shrimp and cook and stir about 5 minutes or until shrimp turn pink. Season to taste with salt substitute and pepper.

3. To serve, spoon ½ cup (120 ml) cooked grits on each plate. Spoon shrimp-green onion mixture evenly over grits and sprinkle with cheese.

Yield: 5 to 6 servings   Serving size: ½ cup (120 ml)

Calcium: 213 g   Protein: 21 g   Carbohydrate: 26 g
Fat: 2 g   Cholesterol: 138 mg   Sodium: 145 mg
Calcium: 58 mg   Fiber: less than 1 g   Sugars: less than 1 g
Sugar Alcohol: 0 g

Food Exchanges: 2 bread, 2 lean meat

■ ■ ■

Breakfast-Bacon Scramble

Net Carbs: 2 g

¼ **cup Egg Beaters® egg substitute**	**60 ml**
2 tablespoons low-fat small curd cottage cheese, drained	**30 ml**
1 teaspoon Smart Balance® buttery spread	**5 ml**
1 slice turkey bacon, cooked, crumbled	

1. Mix egg substitute and cottage cheese. Season to taste with salt substitute and pepper.

2. In sprayed skillet over medium heat, melt buttery spread and heat until it bubbles.

3. Stir in egg mixture and cook and stir until eggs are soft-scrambled. Remove from skillet and drain if needed.

4. Sprinkle with crumbled turkey bacon and serve immediately.

Optional: Add 2 to 3 dashes hot pepper sauce.

Yield: 1 serving   Serving size: ⅓ cup (80 ml)

Calories: 112   Protein: 12 g   Carbohydrate: 2 g
Fat: 6 g   Cholesterol: 12 mg   Sodium: 450 mg
Calcium: 40 mg   Fiber: 0 g   Sugars: less than 1 g
Sugar Alcohol: 0 g

Food Exchanges: ½ medium fat meat, ½ fat

*Egg substitutes are made mostly from egg whites, contain
less fat than whole eggs, and have no cholesterol. Use
1/4 cup (60 ml) refrigerated egg substitute for 1 whole egg.*

Southern Brunch Ham and Rice

Net Carbs: 18 g

This recipe is an excellent way to use leftover rice.

2 cups frozen seasoning blend (celery, onion, peppers, parsley)	**480 ml**
8 slices 98% fat-free deli ham, diced	
2 cups cooked long grain white or brown rice	**480 ml**
½ cup Egg Beaters® egg substitute	**120 ml**

1. To non-stick skillet over medium heat, add 1 to 2 tablespoons (15 - 30 ml) water and frozen seasoning blend. Cook and stir until vegetables are tender, adding more water if needed. Continue cooking and stirring until liquid evaporates.

2. Spray vegetables and skillet with nonstick cooking spray. Add ham and cook 1 to 2 minutes.

3. Stir in rice and mix well. Pour in egg substitute and continue to cook and stir until it sets. Season to taste with salt substitute and pepper.

4. Serve warm.

Yield: 6 servings (about 3 cups/710 ml)   Serving size: ½ cup (120 ml)

Calories: 110	Protein: 6 g	Carbohydrate: 18 g
Fat: less than 1 g	Cholesterol: 8 mg	Sodium: 200 mg
Calcium: 12 mg	Fiber: less than 1 g	Sugars: 2 g
Sugar Alcohol: 0 g		

Food Exchanges: 2 bread, 1 vegetable

■ ■ ■

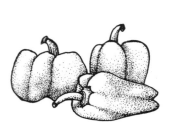

Cheesy Southern Grits

Net Carbs: 14 g

1¾ cups Swanson Natural Goodness® chicken broth	420 ml
½ cup quick-cooking grits	120 ml
¼ cup Egg Beaters® egg substitute	60 ml
1 cup finely shredded reduced-fat cheddar cheese	240 ml

1. Preheat oven to 325° (162°C).

2. In medium saucepan, heat broth until it boils. Slowly stir grits into boiling broth. Reduce heat to simmer, then cover and cook 5 minutes. Remove from heat.

3. While stirring, slowly add Egg Beaters® to grits and mix well. Add shredded cheese and stir until cheese melts.

4. Spray 1-quart (1 L) baking dish with non-stick spray, then add grits. Bake for 30 to 35 minutes and let stand 5 minutes before serving.

Optional: Sprinkle grits with paprika for color.

Yield: 4 servings   Serving size: ½ cup (120 ml)

Calories: 261   Protein: 18 g   Carbohydrate: 15 g
Fat: 14 g   Cholesterol: 40 mg   Sodium: 683 mg
Calcium: 410 mg   Fiber: 1 g   Sugars: less than 1 g
Sugar Alcohol: 0 g

Food Exchanges: 1½ medium fat meat, 1 bread, ½ fat

■ ■ ■

5-Minute Quesadilla Breakfast

Net Carbs: 10 g

2 (8 inch) low-carb whole wheat tortillas	2 (20 cm)
2 tablespoons reduced-fat cream cheese (Neufchatel)	30 ml
1 tablespoon light sugar-free orange marmalade or other fruit spread	15 ml

1. Preheat oven or toaster oven to 400° (202 ° C). On each tortilla, spread 1 tablespoon (15 ml) cream cheese almost to edges. Spread marmalade on top of cream cheese. Fold each tortilla in half. Heat in oven 3 to 4 minutes or until cream cheese begins to melt.

Yield: 2 servings   Serving size: 1 tortilla

Calories: 156   Protein: 7 g   Carbohydrate: 21 g
Fat: 6 g   Cholesterol: 10 mg   Sodium: 390 mg
Calcium: 10 mg   Fiber: 11 g   Sugars: less than 1 g
Sugar Alcohol: 0 g   Food Exchanges: 1½ bread, 1½ other carb, 1 fat

■ ■ ■

Southwest Breakfast Wrap

Net Carbs: 5 g

½ cup southwestern-style Egg Beaters® egg substitute	120 ml
2 (8 inch) low-carb whole wheat tortillas	2 (20 cm)
¼ cup shredded reduced-fat cheddar cheese	60 ml
2 teaspoons chunky salsa	10 ml

1. In non-stick skillet, scramble egg substitute according to package directions. Spread ½ scrambled eggs on each tortilla. Top with cheese and salsa. Roll up, heat in microwave 10 to 15 seconds and serve immediately.

Yield: 2 servings   Serving size: 1 wrap

Calories: 192   Protein: 17 g   Carbohydrate: 8 g
Fat: 11 g   Cholesterol: 20 mg   Sodium: 579 mg
Calcium: 223 mg   Fiber: 3 g   Sugars: less than 1 g
Sugar Alcohol: 0 g   Food Exchanges: 1 fat, ½ bread, ½ medium fat meat

Whole Wheat Banana Pancakes

Net Carbs: 21 g

1 cup whole wheat pancake mix	**240 ml**
¼ cup Egg Beaters® egg substitute	**60 ml**
½ banana, mashed	
2 teaspoons canola oil	**10 ml**

1. Combine all ingredients. Add 1 cup water (240 ml) and mix well. Preheat sprayed non-stick skillet over medium heat until water droplets sizzle and bounce.

2. Spoon 2 tablespoons (30 ml) pancake batter into skillet for each pancake. Cook until pancake browns on each side. Remove each batch and keep warm until serving time.

Optional: Serve with sugar-free breakfast syrup or Maple Syrup Stir-Fry Apples (p. 149).

Yield: About 10 to 12 (3 inch/8 cm) pancakes   Serving size: 2 pancakes
Calories: 131   Protein: 5 g   Carbohydrate: 24 g
Fat: 2 g   Cholesterol: 0 mg   Sodium: 519 mg
Calcium: 53 mg   Fiber: 3 g   Sugars: 5 g
Sugar Alcohol: 0 g   Food Exchanges: 1½ bread, 1½ fruit, ½ fat

⅔ Wide-Awake Wrap

Net Carbs: 5 g

½ cup Egg Beaters® egg substitute	**120 ml**
2 (8 inch) low-carb whole wheat tortillas	**2 (20 cm)**
2 slices turkey bacon, cooked, crumbled	
¼ cup shredded reduced-fat cheddar cheese	**60 ml**

1. In sprayed skillet over medium heat, scramble egg substitute according to package directions.

2. On each tortilla, spread ½ scrambled eggs and ½ crumbled bacon. Sprinkle with cheese. Roll up and heat in microwave 10 to 15 seconds. Serve immediately.

Yield: 2 servings   Serving size: 1 wrap
Calories: 221   Protein: 19 g   Carbohydrate: 8 g
Fat: 14 g   Cholesterol: 30 mg   Sodium: 757 mg
Calcium: 222 mg   Fiber: 3 g   Sugars: less than 1 g
Sugar Alcohol: 0 g   Food Exchanges: 1½ fat, 1 medium fat meat, ½ bread

Buttery Cinnamon Toast

Net Carbs: 9 g

4 slices sugar-free whole wheat bread	
4 teaspoons Smart Balance® buttery spread	**20 ml**
1 tablespoon Splenda® sugar substitute	**15 ml**
½ tablespoon ground cinnamon	**7 ml**

1. Toast bread. Spread each slice with 1 teaspoon (5 ml) buttery spread. In small bowl, combine sugar substitute and cinnamon. Sprinkle over warm toast. Serve immediately.

Yield: 4 servings
Calories: 77
Fat: 2 g
Calcium: 14 mg
Sugar Alcohol: 0 g

Serving size: 1 slice
Protein: 3 g
Cholesterol: 0 mg
Fiber: 3 g
Food Exchanges: ½ bread, ½ fat

Carbohydrate: 12 g
Sodium: 149 mg
Sugars: less than 1 g

■ ■ ■

Deluxe Breakfast Toast

Net Carbs: 9 g

1 tablespoon Splenda® sugar substitute	**15 ml**
¼ teaspoon ground cinnamon	**1 ml**
2 slices reduced-calorie or sugar-free whole wheat bread	
¼ cup low-fat cottage cheese, drained, divided	**60 ml**

1. In small bowl, mix sugar substitute and cinnamon and set aside. Lightly toast bread, then spread each slice with half cottage cheese. Sprinkle tops with cinnamon mixture.

2. Place toast under heated broiler for 1 to 2 minutes or until hot. Serve immediately.

Yield: 2 servings
Calories: 67
Fat: less than 1 g
Calcium: 39 mg
Sugar Alcohol: 0 g

Serving size: 1 slice toast
Protein: 6 g
Cholesterol: 1 mg
Fiber: 3 g
Food Exchanges: 1 bread, ½ lean meat

Carbohydrate: 12 g
Sodium: 232 mg
Sugars: 1 g

❧ French Toast Sticks

Net Carbs: 10 g

4 slices sugar-free whole wheat bread	
½ cup Egg Beaters® egg substitute	**120 ml**
1 tablespoon Splenda® sugar substitute	**15 ml**
½ tablespoon cinnamon	**7 ml**

1. Preheat non-stick skillet over high heat.

2. Cut each slice bread into 3 sticks.

3. Pour egg substitute into shallow dish. In batches, coat bread sticks on both sides with egg substitute and place immediately in skillet.

4. Cook bread on both sides until it browns. Remove and place on serving plate.

5. In small bowl, combine sugar substitute and cinnamon. Sprinkle over warm toast and serve immediately.

Optional: To reduce carbs, prepare with low-carb wheat bread.

Yield: 4 servings (12 sticks) Serving size: 3 sticks

Calories: 85 Protein: 6 g Carbohydrate: 13 g
Fat: 1 g Cholesterol: 0 mg Sodium: 172 mg
Calcium: 21 mg Fiber: 3 mg Sugars: less than 1 g
Sugar Alcohol: 0 g Food Exchanges: 1 bread, ½ lean meat

One ounce (28 g) cornflakes has more sodium than 1 ounce (28 g) salted peanuts.

English Muffin Breakfast
Net Carbs: 19 g

1 whole wheat English muffin halved

4 tablespoons low-fat small curd cottage cheese,
    well drained or part-skim ricotta cheese   **60 ml**

½ cup unsweetened applesauce   **120 ml**

½ to 1 teaspoon ground cinnamon   **2 - 5 ml**

1. Lightly toast muffin halves.

2. Top with cottage cheese and applesauce and sprinkle with cinnamon.

3. Broil 2 to 3 minutes until cheese and applesauce heat through.

4. Serve immediately.

Optional: To reduce carbs, substitute 1 or 2 (8 inch/20 cm) low-carb tortillas for English muffin.

Yield: 2 servings   Serving size: 1 muffin half

Calories: 120   Protein: 7 g   Carbohydrate: 22 g
Fat: 1 g   Cholesterol: 2 mg   Sodium: 327 mg
Calcium: 114 mg   Fiber: 3 g   Sugars: 9 g
Sugar Alcohol: 0 g

Food Exchanges: 1 bread, ½ fruit, ½ lean meat

■ ■ ■

Salads & Dressings

Apple-Zucchini Green Salad

Net Carbs: 10 g

6 cups torn green or red leaf lettuce	**1.5 L**
2 cups unpeeled, cored, coarsely chopped red apple	**480 ml**
1 cup unpeeled thinly sliced zucchini	**240 ml**
2 to 3 tablespoons Green Salad Vinaigrette (p. 67)	
** or olive oil and vinegar**	**30 - 45 ml**

1. In salad bowl, toss lettuce, apple and zucchini.

2. Drizzle vinaigrette over salad and lightly toss. Serve immediately.

Yield: 6 servings   Serving size: 1 cup (240 ml)

Calories: 57	Protein: 2 g	Carbohydrate: 13 g
Fat: less than 1 g	Cholesterol: 0 mg	Sodium: 6 mg
Calcium: 31 mg	Fiber: 3 g	Sugars: 9 g
Sugar Alcohol: 0 g	Food Exchanges: 1 fruit, ½ vegetable	

■ ■ ■

Orange Red-Onion Salad

Net Carbs: 7 g

2 large navel oranges, peeled, sliced	
8 thin red onion slices	
6 cups bite-size romaine or leaf lettuce	**1.5 L**
4 to 5 tablespoons vinaigrette dressing	**60 - 75 ml**

1. Quarter orange slices and place in salad bowl with red onion and lettuce.

2. Toss with vinaigrette and serve immediately.

Yield: 6 servings   Serving size: 1 cup (240 ml)

Calories (without dressing): 40	Protein: 1 g	Carbohydrate: 10 g
Fat: less than 1 g	Cholesterol: 0 mg	Sodium: 5.3 mg
Calcium: 44 mg	Dietary Fiber: 3 g	Sugars: 6 g
Sugar Alcohol: 0 g		

Avocado-Grapefruit Salad

Net Carbs: 7 g

4 cups shredded romaine or leaf lettuce	**.9 L**
1 avocado, peeled, seeded	
1 grapefruit, peeled, sectioned	
2 to 3 tablespoons vinaigrette dressing	**30 - 45 ml**

1. On each of 4 salad plates, place 1 cup (240 ml) shredded lettuce. Slice avocado in ¼-inch (.6 cm) wedges. Arrange wedges and grapefruit sections on lettuce. Drizzle with dressing and serve immediately.

Tip: One head of lettuce yields about 8 cups(1.9 L) shredded lettuce.

Yield: 4 servings
Calories (without dressing): 106
Fat: 7 g
Calcium: 38 mg
Sugar Alcohol: 0 g

Serving size: 1 individual salad
Protein: 2 g   Carbohydrate: 12 g
Cholesterol: 0 mg   Sodium: 8 mg
Fiber: 5 g   Sugar: 5 g
Food Exchanges: 1½ fat, ½ vegetable, ½ fruit

5-Minute Italian Green Salad

Net Carbs: 2 g

½ (16 ounce) jar Italian mix giardiniera (cauliflower, carrots, celery, peppers and pickles in vinegar)	**227 g**
1 (10 ounce) package ready-to-eat romaine lettuce	**280 g**
3 to 4 tablespoons Green Salad Vinaigrette (p.67)	**45 - 60 ml**

1. In wire mesh strainer, drain and rinse Italian mix vegetables to remove excess salt. Chill remaining vegetables in jar for later use.

2. In salad bowl, lightly toss lettuce and vegetables. Drizzle with dressing.

Tip: Prepared ready-to-eat romaine lettuce will make this recipe a snap! In 1 (10 ounce/280 g) package of ready-to-eat romaine lettuce, there are 6 to 8 cups/1.5 - 2 L.

Yield: 6 to 8 servings
Calories (without dressing): 16
Fat: less than 1 g
Calcium: 22 mg
Sugar Alcohol: 0 g

Serving size: 1 cup (240 ml)
Protein: less than 1 g   Carbohydrate: 3 g
Cholesterol: 0 mg   Sodium: 368 mg
Fiber: 1 g   Sugars: less than 1 g
Food Exchanges: 0

❧ Pear and Feta Cheese Salad

Net Carbs: 11 g

4 cups mixed field greens or bite-size romaine lettuce	**.9 L**
2 Anjou pears, unpeeled, cut in large chunks	
2 tablespoons crumbled feta or gorgonzola cheese	**30 ml**
2 to 3 tablespoons Balsamic Vinaigrette (p. 65)	**30 - 45 ml**

1. On each of 4 salad plates, place 1 cup (240 ml) greens.

2. Arrange ½ cup (120 ml) pears over greens on each plate and sprinkle feta cheese on top.

3. Drizzle with Balsamic Vinaigrette and serve immediately.

Optional: Sprinkle each salad with 1 tablespoon (15 ml) chopped walnuts or pecans.

Yield: 4 servings   Serving size: 1 cup (240 ml)

Calories (without dressing): 70   Protein: 2 g   Carbohydrate: 15 g
Fat: 1 g   Cholesterol: 4 mg   Sodium: 62 mg
Calcium: 44 mg   Dietary Fiber: 4 g   Sugars: 9 g
Sugar Alcohol: 0 g

Food Exchanges: 1 fruit, ½ vegetable

◆

Keeping Lettuce Crisp

You will want plenty of lettuce or other greens ready at a moment's notice. Washing and storing lettuce properly will make a big difference in how long it will stay salad-fresh. Remove any bruised, wilted or brown-edged pieces. Separate leaves and wash under cold running water. Use a salad spinner to dry the lettuce, breaking large pieces to fit in the spinner. Layer dry leaves between paper towels and store in zippered plastic bag. Should keep 5 to 7 days. When ready to serve green salad, tear your fresh lettuce and toss with ingredients at the last minute.

Warm Field Greens Salad

Net Carbs: 1 g

1 (10 ounce) package fresh mixed field greens or spinach	**280 ml**
¼ cup chopped green onions with tops	**60 ml**
2 hard-boiled egg whites, chopped	
Sweet-Sour Salad Dressing (p. 66)	

1. In salad bowl, combine greens, green onions and egg whites. In small saucepan, heat salad dressing until it boils. Immediately pour over salad and toss.

Optional: Add 2 tablespoons (30 ml) crumbled feta or gorgonzola cheese.

Yield: 4 servings   Serving size: 1 cup (240 ml)

Calories (without dressing): 23	Protein: 3 g	Carbohydrate: 3 g
Fat: less than 1 g	Cholesterol: 0 mg	Sodium: 41 mg
Calcium: 22 mg	Fiber: 2 g	Sugars: 1 g
Sugar Alcohol: 0 g		

Food Exchanges: ½ very lean meat

■ ■ ■

Tomorrow's Layered Salad

Net Carbs: 4 g

1 head iceberg lettuce, shredded	
1 cup sliced celery	**240 ml**
1 cup frozen green peas, partially thawed	**240 ml**
¾ cup light mayonnaise	**180 ml**

1. In large salad bowl, layer lettuce, celery and peas. Spread mayonnaise to cover and seal top of salad. Cover tightly and chill several hours or until next day. Do not toss.

Yield: 6 servings (6 to 8 cups/1.5 - 1.9 L)   Serving size: 1 cup (240 ml)

Calories: 110	Protein: 2 g	Carbohydrate: 6 g
Fat: 9 g	Cholesterol: 9 mg	Sodium: 244 mg
Calcium: 22 mg	Fiber: 2 g	Sugars: 2 g
Sugar Alcohol: 0 g		

Food Exchanges: 2 fat, ½ vegetable

Creamy Cabbage Slaw

Net Carbs: 2 g

6 cups shredded green cabbage	**1.5 L**
¼ cup chopped green bell pepper	**60 ml**
¼ cup sliced green onions with tops	**60 ml**
⅓ cup Creamy Slaw Dressing (p. 67)	**80 ml**

1. In salad bowl, combine cabbage, bell pepper and green onion. Cover and chill.

2. Just before serving, lightly toss cabbage mixture with dressing and serve immediately.

Yield: 6 to 8 servings   Serving size: ¾ cup (180 ml)

Calories (without dressing): 17   Protein: less than 1 g   Carbohydrate: 4 g
Fat: less than 1 g   Cholesterol: 0 mg   Sodium: 12 mg
Calcium: 31 mg   Fiber: 2 g   Sugar: 2 g
Sugar Alcohol: 0 g
Food Exchanges: 0

■ ■ ■

Fancy Carrot Salad

Net Carbs: 7 g

3 carrots, peeled, coarsely grated	
1 (8 ounce) can crushed pineapple, well drained	**20 cm**
4 tablespoons chopped pecans	**60 ml**
2 to 3 tablespoons light or fat-free mayonnaise	**30 - 45 ml**

1. In salad bowl, combine all ingredients.

2. Chill before serving.

Yield: 6 to 8 servings   Serving size: ½ cup (120 ml)

Calories: 63   Protein: less than 1 g   Carbohydrate: 8 g
Fat: 3 g   Cholesterol: 0 mg   Sodium: 58 mg
Calcium: 11 mg   Fiber: 1 g   Sugars: 5 g
Sugar Alcohol: 0 g
Food Exchanges: ½ fruit, ½ fat

Fiesta Corn Salad

Net Carbs: 9 g

1 (11 ounce) can corn with sweet red and green peppers, drained, rinsed	**312 g**
1 cup low-fat small curd cottage cheese, drained	**240 ml**
⅓ cup chopped green onions with tops	**80 ml**
⅓ cup light sour cream	**80 ml**

1. In mixing bowl, combine corn, cottage cheese and green onions. If needed, strain mixture again to remove excess liquid.

2. Stir in sour cream.

3. Cover and chill before serving.

Yield: 6 to 8 servings
Calories: 81
Fat: 3 g
Calcium: 35 mg
Sugar Alcohol: 0 g
Food Exchanges: ½ milk, ½ fat

Serving size: ½ cup (120 ml)
Protein: 5 g
Cholesterol: 9 mg
Fiber: 1 g

Carbohydrate: 10 g
Sodium: 281 mg
Sugars: 2 g

Crunchy Veggie Salad

Net Carbs: 2 g

½ cup sliced radishes	**120 ml**
½ cup sliced celery	**120 ml**
1 cup sliced zucchini	**240 ml**
2 to 3 tablespoons Classic French Dressing (p. 64) or oil and vinegar	**30 - 45 ml**

1. In salad bowl, mix radishes, celery and zucchini and chill.

2. Just before serving, drizzle salad with dressing and lightly toss.

Yield: 4 servings
Calories (without dressing): 19
Fat: less than 1 g
Calcium: 27 mg
Sugar Alcohol: 0 g
Food Exchanges: 0

Serving size: ½ cup (120 ml)
Protein: 2 g
Cholesterol: 0 mg
Fiber: 1 g

Carbohydrate: 3 g
Sodium: 30 mg
Sugars: 2 g

Warm Three-Bean Salad

Net Carbs: 0 g

2 (15 ounce) cans three-bean salad	**2 (425 g)**
1 (8 ounce) can sliced water chestnuts	**227 g**
Sweet-Sour Salad Dressing (p. 66)	
2 tablespoons bacon bits	**30 ml**

1. Drain cans of three-bean salad and water chestnuts and rinse thoroughly in cold water to remove excess sodium. Place in large ovenproof bowl.

2. Heat Sweet-Sour Salad Dressing (p. 66) and pour over bean mixture. Sprinkle bacon bits on top (do not stir). Serve immediately.

Yield: 6 servings (about 3 cups/710 ml)   Serving size: ½ cup (120 ml)

Calories (without dressing): 134   Protein: 3 g   Carbohydrate: 5 g
Fat: less than 1 g   Cholesterol: 26 mg   Sodium: 546 mg
Calcium: 1 mg   Fiber: 5 g   Sugars: 18 mg
Sugar Alcohol: 0 g   Food Exchanges: 0

■ ■ ■

Baby Pea Salad

Net Carbs: 5 g

1 (16 ounce) package frozen petite peas	**.5 kg**
1 cup thinly sliced celery	**240 ml**
¼ cup finely chopped green onions with tops	**60 ml**
⅓ cup Tangy Basil Dressing (p. 68)	**80 ml**

1. Cook peas according to package directions. Do not overcook. Drain and cool slightly. In salad bowl, combine all ingredients. Chill several hours or overnight, stirring occasionally. Drain excess dressing when ready to serve.

Variation: Substitute 1 (15 ounce/425 g) can petite peas, drained, for frozen peas.

Yield: 8 servings   Serving size: ½ cup (120 ml)

Calories (without dressing): 47   Protein: 3 g   Carbohydrate: 8 g
Fat: less than 1 g   Cholesterol: 0 mg   Sodium: 75 mg
Calcium: 6 mg   Fiber: 3 g   Sugars: 4 g
Sugar Alcohol: 0 g   Food Exchanges: ½ vegetable

Greek Salad

Net Carbs: 3 g

2 large tomatoes, cut into wedges
⅓ cup red onion slivers   **80 ml**
8 large pitted black olives, sliced
2 to 3 tablespoons Feta Cheese Dressing, (p. 64)   **30 - 45 ml**

1. In salad bowl, combine tomatoes, red onions and olives. Toss with dressing and serve immediately.

Yield: 6 servings (about 3 cups/710 ml)   Serving size: ½ cup (120 ml)

Calories (without dressing): 18   Protein: less than 1 g   Carbohydrate: 3 g
Fat: less than 1 g   Cholesterol: 0 mg   Sodium: 55 mg
Calcium: 8 mg   Fiber: less than 1 g   Sugars: less than 1 g
Sugar Alcohol: 0 g   Food Exchanges: 0

Italian Green Bean Salad

Net Carbs: 5 g

1 (16 ounce) package frozen cut Italian green beans
    or regular cut green beans   **.5 kg**
2 tablespoons canned diced pimento or
    diced roasted red pepper   **30 ml**
2 tablespoons grated parmesan or romano cheese   **30 ml**
⅓ cup light mayonnaise   **80 ml**

1. Cook green beans according to package directions and drain. Do not overcook.

2. In salad bowl, mix all ingredients. Serve warm or chilled.

Variation: Substitute 4 cups (.9 L) canned cut Italian green beans, drained, rinsed for frozen green beans.

Yield: 8 servings (about 4 cups/.9 L)   Serving size: ½ cup (120 ml)

Calories: 88   Protein: 1 g   Carbohydrate: 7 g
Fat: 7 g   Cholesterol: 8 mg   Sodium: 143 mg
Calcium: 42 mg   Fiber: 2 g   Sugars: 2 g
Sugar Alcohol: 0 g   Food Exchanges: 1½ fat, ½ vegetable

Cauliflower-Olive Salad

Net Carbs: 1 g

1 (12 ounce) head raw cauliflower	340 g
¼ cup sliced black olives, drained	60 ml
¼ cup diced pimentos, drained	60 ml
2 to 3 tablespoons Classic French Dressing (p. 64) or oil and vinegar	30 - 45 ml

1. Wash cauliflower and remove leaves and woody stems. Separate cauliflower into florets.

2. Transfer florets to small saucepan and cover with about 1 inch (2.5 cm) water. Cover and boil 8 to 10 minutes or until cauliflower is crisp tender. (To cook in microwave, place raw florets in covered dish with 2 tablespoons (30 ml) water. Cook on HIGH for 5 to 6 minutes or just until cauliflower is crisp tender.)

3. Drain cooked florets and cool 10 to 15 minutes.

4. In salad bowl, mix cauliflower, olives and pimentos. Toss lightly with 2 to 3 tablespoons (30 - 45 ml) Classic French Dressing. Season to taste with salt substitute and pepper.

5. Serve on lettuce leaf or toss with salad greens.

Tip: One head cauliflower yields about 3 cups (710 ml) florets.

Yield: 6 servings (About 3 ½ cups/830 ml)   Serving size: ½ cup (120 ml)

Calories (without dressing): 21	Protein: 1 g	Carbohydrate: 3 g
Fat: less than 1 g	Cholesterol: 0 mg	Sodium: 66 mg
Calcium: 17 mg	Dietary Fiber: 2 g	Sugars: 1 g
Sugar Alcohol: 0 g		

Food Exchanges: 0

◆

Cut Down on Salad Dressing

When you prepare a green salad, place added ingredients such as diced tomato, avocado, green onions, etc., in a bowl together. Measure recommended portion of salad dressing and drizzle over the bowl of vegetables and stir gently. When ready to serve salad, spoon on salad dressing mixture and toss gently. No need to add more dressing!

Artichoke-Red Pepper Salad

Net Carbs: 3 g

1 (6 ounce) jar marinated artichoke hearts	168 g
½ cup slivered red bell pepper	120 ml
¼ cup slivered white or yellow onion	60 ml
1 head torn romaine lettuce or torn fresh spinach	

1. Drain artichoke hearts and reserve marinade.

2. Coarsely chop artichoke hearts and place in mixing bowl. Add red bell pepper and onions.

3. Add 2 tablespoons (30 ml) reserved marinade and stir. Cover and chill.

4. Place lettuce in salad bowl and add marinated vegetables. Toss to lightly coat lettuce. Serve immediately.

Optional: You may substitute green bell pepper for red bell pepper. You may substitute canned roasted red pepper or ¼ cup (60 ml) drained sliced pimentos for the fresh bell pepper.

Yield: 8 servings   Serving size: 1 cup (240 ml)

Calories: 47
Fat: 4 g
Calcium: 20 mg
Sugar Alcohol: 0 g

Protein: less than 1 g
Cholesterol: 0 mg
Fiber: 1 g

Carbohydrate: 4 g
Sodium: 78 mg
Sugars: 1 g

Food Exchanges: 1 fat

◆

*If your lettuce or greens have passed the peak of freshness,
they will still taste great when cooked as wilted.*

57

Chicken-Pasta Salad

Net Carbs: 17 g

1 (16 to 20 ounce) package frozen vegetable blend	.5 kg - 624 g
1½ cups cooked reduced-carb pasta	360 ml
2 broiled boneless, skinless chicken breasts, cubed	
2 to 3 teaspoons Sesame Seed Dressing (p. 66)	30 - 45 ml

1. Cook vegetables according to package directions. Do not overcook. Drain. In salad bowl, combine all ingredients and lightly toss. Season to taste with salt substitute and pepper.

Tip: The vegetable blend with mushrooms, broccoli and squash is really good. Try rotini, shells or macaroni for pasta.

Yield: 4 servings
Calories (without dressing): 234
Fat: 2 g
Calcium: 28 mg
Sugar Alcohol: 0 g

Serving size: ½ to ¾ cup (120 - 180 ml)
Protein: 26 g   Carbohydrate: 26 g
Cholesterol: 43 mg   Sodium: 312 mg
Fiber: 9 g   Sugars: 4 g
Food Exchanges: 3 bread, 2 very lean meat, 2 vegetable

■ ■ ■

❧ Oriental Chicken Slaw

Net Carbs: 14 g

1 (3 ounce) package ramen noodles, crushed	84 g
½ cup diced cooked chicken breast	120 ml
4 cups shredded cabbage or coleslaw mix	.9 L
2 to 3 tablespoons Sesame Seed Dressing (p. 66) or oil and vinegar	30 - 45 ml

1. In dry skillet over medium heat, cook and stir noodles until they turn light brown. Stir constantly to avoid burning.

2. In salad bowl, combine toasted noodles, chicken and cabbage.

3. Drizzle with 2 tablespoons (30 ml) Sesame Seed Dressing. Toss lightly and serve immediately.

Yield: 4 servings
Calories (without dressing): 140
Fat: 5 g
Calcium: 33 mg
Sugar Alcohol: 0 g

Serving size: 1½ cups
Protein: 8 g   Carbohydrate: 16 g
Cholesterol: 12 mg   Sodium: 549 mg
Fiber: 2 g   Sugars: 3 g
Food Exchanges: 1 bread, ½ meat, ½ vegetable

❧ Classic Tuna Salad

Net Carbs: 5 g

1 (6 ounce) can solid white albacore tuna in water	**168 G**
2 tablespoons light or fat-free mayonnaise	**30 ml**
1 red apple, unpeeled, diced	
½ cup diced celery	**120 ml**

1. Drain tuna and break up with fork. Transfer to salad bowl. Add mayonnaise, apple and celery. Toss lightly to mix.

Optional: Add ¼ cup (60 ml) chopped pecans.

Yield: 4 servings   Serving size: ½ cup (120 ml)

Calories: 86   Protein: 11 g   Carbohydrate: 6 g
Fat: 2 g   Cholesterol: 19 mg   Sodium: 269 mg
Calcium: 12 mg   Fiber: 1 g   Sugars: 4 g
Sugar Alcohol: 0 g   Food Exchanges: 1½ lean meat, 1 fruit, 1 vegetable

■ ■ ■

Curried Fruit and Chicken Salad

Net Carbs: 6 g

¼ teaspoon curry powder	**1 ml**
2 tablespoons light mayonnaise, divided	**30 ml**
2 cups diced cooked, boneless, skinless chicken breasts	**480 ml**
1 cup seedless red or green grapes, halved	**240 ml**

1. In mixing bowl, combine curry powder and 1 tablespoon (15 ml) mayonnaise. Add chicken and grapes and mix. If needed to moisten ingredients, add remaining 1 tablespoon (15 ml) mayonnaise.

Yield: 6 servings   Serving size: ¼ cup (60 ml)
Calories: 112   Protein: 15 g   Carbohydrate: 6 g
Fat: 3 g   Cholesterol: 41 mg   Sodium: 65 mg
Calcium: 10 mg   Fiber: less than 1 g   Sugars: 4 g
Sugar Alcohol: 0 g   Food Exchanges: ½ lean meat, ½ fruit, ½ fat

*Starchy vegetables such as corn, peas, and potatoes are found
on the starch rather than vegetable Exchange List.*

Tuna Salad Tomato Cups

Net Carbs: 5 g

3 large firm ripe tomatoes	
1 (6 ounce) can solid white albacore tuna in water, **drained**	**165 g**
⅓ cup light mayonnaise	**80 ml**
½ cup chopped celery	**120 ml**

1. Cut off about ⅓ of stem end of each tomato. Carefully scoop out tomato pulp and save for later use or discard.

2. In mixing bowl, mix tuna, mayonnaise and celery. Season to taste with salt substitute and pepper. Mound ⅓ tuna mixture in each tomato cup and serve.

Optional: Add 1 tablespoon (15 ml) dill or sweet pickle relish to tuna mixture.

Yield: 3 servings
Calories: 182
Fat: 10 g
Calcium: 21 mg
Sugar Alcohol: 0 g
Serving size: 1 tomato cup
Protein: 16 g
Cholesterol: 34 mg
Fiber: 2 g
Carbohydrate: 7 g
Sodium: 478 mg
Sugars: 3 g
Food Exchanges: 2 medium fat meat, 1 other carb, ½ vegetable

On-the-Go Shrimp Salad

Net Carbs: 2 g

4 cups shredded iceberg lettuce	**.9 L**
1 large firm ripe tomato	
½ pound frozen cooked shrimp, thawed	**227 g**
2 to 4 tablespoons Lemon Oil Dressing (p. 144) **or oil and vinegar**	**30 - 60 ml**

1. On each of 4 salad plates, place 1 cup (240 ml) lettuce. Top with tomato wedges and shrimp. Drizzle 1 tablespoon (15 ml) dressing on each. Serve immediately.

Tip: You could also use 2 to 3 Roma (pear) tomatoes, cut in wedges.

Yield: 4 servings
Calories (without dressing): 67
Fat: less than 1 g
Calcium: 36 mg
Sugar Alcohol: 0 g
Serving size: 1½ cups (360 ml)
Protein: 13 g
Cholesterol: 111 mg
Fiber: less than 1 g
Carbohydrate: 2 g
Sodium: 133 mg
Sugars: 2 g
Food Exchanges: ½ very lean meat

Potluck Peach Salad

Net Carbs: 8 g

2 (.3 ounce) packages sugar-free peach gelatin mix	2 (12 g)
1 (20 ounce) can pineapple tidbits and juice	624 g
2 red apples, unpeeled, cored, diced	
½ cup chopped pecans	120 ml

1. In saucepan, heat 2 cups water (480 ml) until it boils. Add gelatin and stir until it dissolves. Combine pineapple juice only and enough water to equal 1 cup (240 ml). Stir into dissolved gelatin. Pour mixture into 9 x 13-inch (23 x 33 cm) dish and chill until it begins to thicken. Stir in pineapple, apples and pecans and chill until gelatin sets.

Optional: Serve with reduced-fat or fat-free whipped topping.

Yield: 12 to 14 servings
Calories: 64
Fat: 3 g
Calcium: 4 mg
Sugar Alcohol: 0 g
Food Exchanges: ½ fruit, ½ fat

Serving size: ½ cup (120 ml)
Protein: less than 1 g
Cholesterol: 0 mg
Fiber: 1 g

Carbohydrate: 9 g
Sodium: 33 mg
Sugars: 7 g

■ ■ ■

Green Light Gelatin

Net Carbs: 7 g

1 (.3 ounce) package sugar-free lime gelatin mix	12 g
1 (8 ounce) can crushed pineapple in juice with liquid	227 g
2 tablespoons light mayonnaise	30 ml
1 cup low-fat small curd cottage cheese, drained	240 ml

1. In saucepan, heat 1 cup (240 ml) water until it boils. Add gelatin mix and stir until it dissolves. Add crushed pineapple with juice and mayonnaise and mix. Stir in cottage cheese and mix well. Pour into 1-quart (1 L) square dish and chill until gelatin sets.

Yield: 6 servings
Calories: 78
Fat: 2 g
Calcium: 26 mg
Sugar Alcohol: 0 g

Serving size: About ½ cup (120 ml)
Protein: 6 g
Cholesterol: 5 mg
Fiber: less than 1 g
Food Exchanges: 1 lean meat, ½ fruit, ½ other carb

Carbohydrate: 7 g
Sodium: 227 mg
Sugars: 5 g

❧ Pineapple-Blueberry Gelatin Salad

Net Carbs: 7 g

2 (.3 ounce) packages sugar-free raspberry or cranberry gelatin mix	**2 (12 g)**
1½ cups fresh or frozen blueberries	**360 ml**
1 (8 ounce) can crushed pineapple with juice	**227 g**
1 (8 ounce) carton lite whipped topping, thawed	**227 g**

1. In saucepan, heat 2 cups (480 ml) water until it boils. Add gelatin and stir until it dissolves.

2. In mixing bowl, combine blueberry syrup, pineapple juice and enough water to equal 1 cup (240 ml). Stir into gelatin mixture. Set aside ½ cup (120 ml) gelatin mixture.

3. Add pineapple and blueberries to gelatin and mix well.

4. Pour gelatin into 9 x 13-inch (23 x 33 cm) dish. Chill several hours or until gelatin sets.

5. Fold ½ cup (120 ml) reserved gelatin mixture into 1 cup (240 ml) whipped topping. Lightly fold in remaining whipped topping. Spread over firm gelatin. Chill before serving.

Tip: One (15 ounce/425 g) can blueberries in light syrup with juice will also work in this recipe.

Yield: 16 servings (About 8 cups/2.9 L) Serving size: ½ cup (120 ml)
Calories: 53   Protein: less than 1 g   Carbohydrate: 7 g
Fat: 2 g   Cholesterol: 0 mg   Sodium: 25 mg
Calcium: 2 mg   Fiber: less than 1 g   Sugars: 5 g
Sugar Alcohol: 0 g
Food Exchanges: 0

◆

Fruit canned in extra-light syrup generally has the same grams of carbohydrate per serving as does fruit canned in juice. Not so for fruit canned in heavy syrup!

Perfection Gelatin Mold

Net Carbs: 2 g

2 (.3 ounce) packages sugar-free lemon gelatin mix	**2 (12 g)**
2 cups finely shredded or chopped green cabbage	**480 ml**
1 cup grated carrot	**240 ml**
1 cup chopped celery	**240 ml**

1. In saucepan, heat 2 cups (480 ml) water until it boils. Stir in gelatin and stir until it dissolves. Transfer to large bowl and chill gelatin until it thickens, about 45 to 60 minutes.

2. Carefully fold remaining ingredients into thickened gelatin. Pour gelatin into sprayed 6-cup (1.5 L) ring mold.

3. Chill until firm, about 4 hours or overnight. Remove gelatin salad from mold onto serving plate.

Yield: 12 servings   Serving size: ½ cup (120 ml)

Calories: 9   Protein: less than 1 g   Carbohydrate: 2 g
Fat: less than 1 g   Cholesterol: 0 mg   Sodium: 21 mg
Calcium: 11 mg   Fiber: less than 1 g   Sugars: less than 1 g
Sugar Alcohol: 0 g

Food Exchanges: 0

---

*A "free" food is any food or drink with 20 calories
or less and 5 grams carbs or less per serving.*

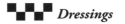

Classic French Dressing

Net Carbs: less than 1 g

½ cup canola, peanut, or olive oil	120 ml
¼ cup white wine or rice vinegar	60 ml
1 teaspoon dry mustard or dijon-style mustard	5 ml
1 teaspoon ground paprika	5 ml

1. Combine all ingredients in bottle or jar with lid. Season to taste with salt substitute and pepper.

2. Shake well. Shake again before serving.

Yield: 12 servings (About ¾ cup/180 ml)

Serving size: 2 teaspoons (10 ml)

Calories: 83
Fat: 9 g
Calcium: 1 mg
Sugar Alcohol: 0 g

Protein: less than 1 g
Cholesterol: 0 mg
Fiber: less than 1 g
Food Exchanges: 2 fat

Carbohydrate: less than 1 g
Sodium: 10 mg
Sugars: less than 1 g

■ ■ ■

Feta Cheese Dressing

Net Carbs: 2 g

2 tablespoons canola, peanut or olive oil	30 ml
3 tablespoons balsamic vinegar, red wine vinegar or cider vinegar	45 ml
1 tablespoon fresh basil or 1 teaspoon dried basil	15 ml
2 tablespoons crumbled feta cheese	30 ml

1. Combine all ingredients and mix well. Transfer to container with lid.

2. Shake well before using.

Yield: 6 servings (About ½ cup/120 ml)

Serving size: 2 teaspoons (10 ml)

Calories: 58
Fat: 5 g
Calcium: 8 mg
Sugar Alcohol: 0 g

Protein: less than 1 g
Cholesterol: 2 mg
Fiber: less than 1 g
Food Exchanges: 1 fat

Carbohydrate: 2 g
Sodium: 33 mg
Sugars: 2 g

Balsamic Vinaigrette

Net Carbs: 2 g

2 tablespoons canola, peanut or olive oil	**30 ml**
3 tablespoons dark or white balsamic vinegar	**45 ml**
¼ teaspoon dried basil, crushed	**1 ml**
¼ teaspoon dijon-style mustard	**1 ml**

1. In sealed container, mix or shake all ingredients until they blend well.

2. Add ¼ teaspoon (1 ml) black pepper.

3. Shake again before serving.

Yield: 6 servings (about ½ cup/120 ml)   Serving size: 2 tablespoons (30 ml)

Calories: 51	Protein: 0 g	Carbohydrate: 2 g
Fat: 5 g	Cholesterol: 0 mg	Sodium: 6 mg
Calcium: less than 1 mg	Fiber: 0 g	Sugars: 2 g
Sugar Alcohol: 0 g	Food Exchanges: 1 fat	

Distilled white vinegar is made from distilled grain alcohol and has a strong, sour flavor.

Balsamic vinegar is made from white Trebbiano grape juice and aged at least ten years. The vinegar has a slight sweetness, dark brown color and syrupy body. There are a variety of balsamic vinegars now in supermarkets.

Wine vinegars are made from red or white wine and derive flavor from the type of wine used.

Sesame Seed Dressing

Net Carbs: less than 1 g

1 tablespoon sesame seeds	15 ml
2 tablespoons canola, peanut or olive oil	30 ml
2 tablespoons white wine or rice vinegar	30 ml
1 tablespoon lite (reduced sodium) soy sauce	15 ml

1. In dry skillet over medium heat, cook and stir sesame seeds until they turn light brown. Stir constantly to avoid burning.

2. In jar or bottle with lid, combine all ingredients. Shake well to blend. Shake again before serving.

Yield: About 7 servings (About ⅓ cup/80 ml)

Serving size: 2 teaspoons (10 ml)

Calories: 45
Fat: 5 g
Calcium: 14 mg
Sugar Alcohol: 0 g

Protein: less than 1 g
Cholesterol: 0 mg
Fiber: less than 1 g
Food Exchanges: 1 fat

Carbohydrate: less than 1 g
Sodium: 83 mg
Sugars: less than 1 g

■ ■ ■

Sweet-Sour Salad Dressing

Net Carbs: less than 1 g

¼ cup canola oil	60 ml
¼ cup white wine vinegar	60 ml
2 tablespoons Splenda® sugar substitute	30 ml
¼ teaspoon regular or white wine Worcestershire sauce	1 ml

1. Combine ingredients and shake well before using.

Yield: 4 servings (½ cup/120 ml)

Serving size: 2 tablespoons (30 ml)

Calories: 126
Fat: 14 g
Calcium: 1 mg
Sugar Alcohol: 0 g

Protein: 0 g
Cholesterol: 0 mg
Fiber: 0 g
Food Exchanges: 3 fat

Carbohydrate: less than 1 g
Sodium: less than 1 mg
Sugars: less than 1 g

Creamy Slaw Dressing

Net Carbs: 2 g

½ cup light or fat-free mayonnaise	120 ml
1 tablespoon Splenda® sugar substitute	15 ml
1 tablespoon cider vinegar or rice vinegar	15 ml
½ teaspoon celery seed	2 ml

1. In mixing bowl, cream all ingredients and ½ teaspoon (2 ml) salt substitute.

2. Chill in covered container.

Optional: Add 1 to 2 additional teaspoons (5 - 10 ml) vinegar, if desired.

Yield: 12 servings (about ¾ cup/180 ml)

Calories: 34
Fat: 3 g
Calcium: 2 mg
Sugar Alcohol: 0 g

Protein: less than 1 g
Cholesterol: 3 mg
Fiber: less than 1 g
Food Exchanges: ½ fat

Serving size: 2 teaspoons (30 ml)
Carbohydrate: 2 g
Sodium: 60 mg
Sugars: less than 1 g

∎∎∎

Green Salad Vinaigrette

Net Carbs: less than 1 g

3 tablespoons canola, peanut or olive oil	45 ml
2 tablespoons cider vinegar or red wine vinegar or lemon juice	30 ml
1½ teaspoons Splenda® sugar substitute	7 ml

1. In bottle or jar with lid, combine oil, vinegar and sugar substitute with ¼ teaspoon (1 ml) salt substitute and dash freshly ground black pepper.

2. Shake well before using.

Yield: 6 to 7 servings

Serving size: 2 teaspoons (10 ml)

Calories: 61
Fat: 7 g
Calcium: less than 1 mg
Sugar Alcohol: 0 g

Protein: 0 g
Cholesterol: 0 mg
Dietary Fiber: 0 g
Food Exchanges: 1½ fat

Carbohydrate: less than 1 g
Sodium: less than 1 mg
Sugars: less than 1 g

Tangy Basil Dressing

Net Carbs: less than 1 g

¼ **cup apple cider vinegar**	**60 ml**
¼ **cup Splenda® sugar substitute**	**60 ml**
¼ **cup canola, peanut or olive oil**	**60 ml**
1 **teaspoon crushed dried basil**	**5 ml**

1. In small saucepan over medium heat, heat vinegar and sugar substitute until it dissolves. Remove from heat.

2. Add oil, basil and ½ teaspoon (2 ml) salt substitute and mix well. Mix again before serving.

Variation: Substitute dried dillweed for basil.

Yield: About 12 servings (¾ cup/180 ml)

Serving: 1 to 2 teaspoons (5 - 10 ml)

Calories: 41	Protein: 0 g	Carbohydrate: less than 1 g
Fat: 5 g	Cholesterol: 0 mg	Sodium: less than 1 g
Calcium: less than 1 g	Fiber: 0 g	Sugars: less than 1 g
Sugar Alcohol: 0 g		

Food Exchanges: 1 fat

◆

Apple cider vinegar is made from fermented apple cider and has a strong bite with slight apple flavor.

Vegetables & Soups

Asparagus with Garlic and Basil

Net Carbs: 3 g

1½ pounds asparagus, washed, trimmed	**680 g**
2 cloves garlic, minced	
1 teaspoon dried crushed basil or	**5 ml**
1 tablespoon fresh basil, finely chopped	**15 ml**
1 tablespoon lite (reduced sodium) soy sauce	**15 ml**

1. In non-stick large skillet or Dutch oven, heat ⅓ cup (80 ml) water until it boils.

2. Add asparagus, cover and cook over medium heat about 5 minutes or until asparagus is crisp-tender. Uncover and continue to boil about 1 to 2 minutes until water evaporates. Do not overcook. Remove asparagus and keep warm.

3. Spray dry skillet with cooking spray and add garlic and basil. Cook and stir 1 to 2 minutes.

4. Stir in soy sauce and season to taste with black pepper. Pour sauce over cooked asparagus. Serve immediately.

Yield: 6 to 8 servings   Serving size: ½ cup (120 ml)

Calories: 26	Protein: 3 g	Carbohydrate: 5 g
Fat: less than 1 g	Cholesterol: 0 mg	Sodium: 98 mg
Calcium: 30 mg	Fiber: 2 g	Sugars: 2 g
Sugar Alcohol: 0 g		

Food Exchanges: ½ vegetable

Before adding a dried herb to a recipe, crush it between your finger and thumb to help release the herb's flavor. Add it to a recipe at the beginning of cooking to develop flavor.

Oriental Asparagus

Net Carbs: 2 g

1 pound fresh asparagus	**.5 kg**
2 tablespoons lite (reduced sodium) soy sauce	**30 ml**
1 tablespoon cooking sherry	**15 ml**
¼ teaspoon ground ginger	**1 ml**

1. In saucepan, heat 1 inch (2.5 cm) water until it boils. Wash asparagus, remove tough ends and cut in 2-inch (5 cm) lengths. Add asparagus to water and cook until crisp-tender, about 4 to 5 minutes. Do not overcook. Drain and set aside.

2. Mix soy sauce, sherry and ground ginger.

3. In saucepan, combine asparagus and sauce. Cook and stir over medium heat until sauce and asparagus heat through. Serve immediately.

Variation: If you don't want to use cooking sherry, substitute 1 tablespoon (15 ml) Splenda® sugar substitute.

Yield: 8 servings   Serving size: ½ cup (120 ml)

Calories: 17   Protein: 2 g   Carbohydrate: 3 g
Fat: less than 1 g   Cholesterol: 0 mg   Sodium: 156 mg
Calcium: 17 mg   Fiber: 1 g   Sugars: 1 g
Sugar Alcohol: 0 g

Food Exchanges: 0

◆

We should eat 3 to 5 servings of vegetables every day.
Keep plenty of raw, frozen and canned vegetables on
hand so you always have vegetables ready to eat.

Beets in Sweet-Sour Sauce

Net Carbs: 7 g

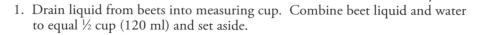

1 (16 ounce) can sliced or whole beets	.5 kg
2 teaspoons corn starch	10 ml
2 tablespoons Splenda® sugar substitute	30 ml
2 tablespoons cider vinegar	30 ml

1. Drain liquid from beets into measuring cup. Combine beet liquid and water to equal ½ cup (120 ml) and set aside.

2. Mix corn starch and sugar substitute. Stir in vinegar and mix well.

3. In saucepan over medium heat, combine corn starch mixture and beet liquid. Heat to boiling and boil 1 to 2 minutes. Stir in beets and cook until they heat through.

Yield: 4 to 6 servings   Serving size: ½ cup (120 ml)

Calories: 31
Fat: 0 g
Calcium: less than 1 mg
Sugar Alcohol: 0 g

Protein: less than 1 g
Cholesterol: 0 mg
Fiber: 1 g

Carbohydrate: 8 g
Sodium: 214 mg
Sugars: 4 g

Food Exchanges: ½ vegetable

To cut down on salt, use fresh and frozen vegetables. Drain and rinse canned vegetables, and look for "no added salt" varieties.

7-Minute Broccoli Stir Fry

Net Carbs: 3 g

1 pound fresh broccoli florets	**.5 kg**
1 (8 ounce) package fresh mushrooms, sliced	**227 g**
2 green onions with tops, sliced	
¼ cup slivered almonds, toasted	**60 ml**

1. Preheat sprayed non-stick wok or skillet on high heat. When hot, add broccoli and stir fry 1 minute.

2. Add 1 tablespoon (15 ml) water, cover and cook, stirring frequently, about 3 minutes or until broccoli is crisp-tender. Add more water if needed. Remove broccoli and set aside.

3. Spray wok with non-stick cooking spray and add mushrooms and green onions. Cook and stir until liquid from mushrooms evaporates, about 3 minutes.

4. Return broccoli to wok, stir and heat mixture until hot. Sprinkle with almonds and serve immediately.

Yield: 6 to 8 servings   Serving size: ¾ cup (180 ml)

Calories: 58   Protein: 4 g   Carbohydrate: 5 g
Fat: 3 g   Cholesterol: 0 mg   Sodium: 18 mg
Calcium: 32 mg   Fiber: 2 g   Sugars: 2 g
Sugar Alcohol: 0 g

Food Exchanges: ½ vegetable, ½ fat

The best way to clean fresh mushrooms is to wipe them with a clean, damp cloth or use a soft mushroom brush. If you wish, lightly rinse and dry immediately. Do not soak fresh mushrooms because it will ruin their texture. To keep mushrooms firm longer, store loose mushrooms or those in an opened package in a paper bag in the refrigerator. Storing in a plastic bag causes quick deterioration.

Better Brussels Sprouts

Net Carbs: 7 g

1 (10 ounce) package frozen brussels sprouts	**280 g**
1 onion, chopped	
1 tomato, seeded, diced, drained	
4 to 5 tablespoons light or fat-free sour cream	**60 - 75 ml**

1. Cook sprouts according to package directions. Set aside and keep warm.

2. In sprayed skillet over medium heat, cook and stir onion until tender. Stir in tomato and cook until it heats through.

3. Stir in tomato, sprouts and salt substitute and pepper to taste.

4. Garnish individual servings with 1 tablespoon (15 ml) sour cream.

Yield: 4 to 5 servings   Serving size: ½ cup (120 ml)

Calories: 66	Protein: 4 g	Carbohydrate: 10 g
Fat: 2 g	Cholesterol: 6 mg	Sodium: 16 mg
Calcium: 43 mg	Fiber: 3 g	Sugars: 2 g
Sugar Alcohol: 0 g		

Food Exchanges: ½ vegetable, ½ fat

Vegetables contribute 1 to 4 grams of fiber per serving.

Cabbage Stir-Fry

Net Carbs: 5 g

1 large onion, thinly sliced	
1 to 2 cloves garlic, finely minced	
1 small head (about 1¼ pounds) green cabbage, shredded	**.7 kg**
1 tablespoon lite (reduced sodium) soy sauce	**15 ml**

1. In sprayed non-stick skillet or wok on medium high heat, cook and stir onion and garlic 2 minutes or until onion is tender.

2. Add shredded cabbage, soy sauce and 1 tablespoon (15 ml) water. Cook and stir 4 minutes or until cabbage is crisp-tender.

3. Serve immediately.

Yield: 6 to 8 servings   Serving size: ¾ cup (180 ml)

Calories: 29	Protein: 2 g	Carbohydrate: 7 g
Fat: less than 1 g	Cholesterol: 0 mg	Sodium: 97 mg
Calcium: 44 mg	Fiber: 2 g	Sugars: 4 g
Sugar Alcohol: 0 g		

Food Exchanges: ½ vegetable

Yellow onions are round or flat in shape, with a mild or sharp flavor. Sweet yellow onions generally have thin, light outer skins, higher water content, and a high sugar content, such as Vidalia onions. They have a fairly short storage life.

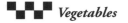

❧ Ratta-Tooey

Net Carbs: 6 g

1 (1 pound) eggplant, peeled, cubed	.5 kg
1 (16 ounce) package frozen seasoning blend (celery, onions, peppers, parsley)	.5 kg
1 zucchini, sliced	
½ cup Carb Options™ garden-style sauce	120 ml

1. In Dutch oven over high heat, add eggplant, seasoning blend, zucchini and 2 tablespoons (30 ml) water. Heat until mixture boils, then reduce heat to low and cover.

2. Cook about 10 to 15 minutes or until vegetables are tender. Drain.

3. Return eggplant mixture to Dutch oven. Add ½ cup (120 ml) pasta sauce and stir until sauce heats through.

4. If desired, season to taste with salt substitute and pepper. Serve hot.

Yield: 6 servings (about 3 cups/710 ml)　　　　Serving size: ½ cup (120 ml)

Calories: 40　　　　Protein: less than 1 g　　　　Carbohydrate: 8 g
Fat: less than 1 g　　Cholesterol: 0 mg　　　　Sodium: 79 mg
Calcium: 8 mg　　　Fiber: 2 g　　　　　　　Sugars: 4 g
Sugar Alcohol: 0 g

Food Exchanges: ½ vegetable

■ ■ ■

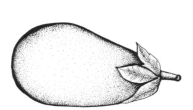

Eggplant-Tomato Casserole

Net Carbs: 7 g

1 (1 to 1¼ pound) eggplant, peeled, cubed	**.5 - .7 kg**
½ cup seasoned breadcrumbs, divided	**120 ml**
½ cup Egg Beaters® egg substitute	**120 ml**
2 tomatoes, sliced	

1. Preheat oven to 350° (176° C). In saucepan, heat 2 inches (5 cm) water until it boils. Add eggplant and cook until it is soft.

2. Drain and mash eggplant with fork. Stir in breadcrumbs, egg substitute, salt substitute and pepper to taste.

3. In sprayed 9 x 9-inch (23 x 23 cm) baking dish, spread eggplant mixture and top with sliced tomatoes. Sprinkle tomatoes with remaining breadcrumbs and coat with cooking spray.

4. Bake uncovered at 350° (176° C) for about 25 to 30 minutes or until tomatoes are tender and light brown around edges.

Optional: Over medium heat, cook and stir ⅓ cup (80 ml) chopped onion and 2 minced garlic cloves until onion is clear and tender. Stir into eggplant mixture.

Yield: 8 servings   Serving size: ½ cup (120 ml)

Calories: 50   Protein: 3 g   Carbohydrate: 10 g
Fat: less than 1 g   Cholesterol: less than 1 g   Sodium: 216 mg
Calcium: 18 mg   Fiber: 3 g   Sugars: 2 g
Sugar Alcohol: 0 g

Food Exchanges: ½ bread

*Few of us get enough dietary fiber. The goal should
be to eat at least 20 grams of fiber a day.*

Oriental Green Beans

Net Carbs: 3 g

1 (16 ounce) package frozen French-style cut green beans	.5 kg
½ cup sliced, rinsed, drained water chestnuts	120 ml
¼ cup chopped green onion with tops	60 ml
2 tablespoons lite (reduced sodium) soy sauce	30 ml

1. Cook green beans according to package directions. Drain.

2. Transfer green beans to medium skillet or saucepan. Add water chestnuts, green onions and soy sauce and mix well. Cook and stir mixture over medium heat until hot. Serve immediately.

Optional: Before serving, sprinkle with chopped salt-free peanuts or toasted, slivered almonds.

Yield: 6 to 8 servings   Serving size: ½ cup (120 ml)

Calories: 26	Protein: 1 g	Carbohydrate: 5 g
Fat: 0 g	Cholesterol: 0 mg	Sodium: 174 mg
Calcium: 21 mg	Fiber: 2 g	Sugars: 2 g
Sugar Alcohol: 0 g		

Food Exchanges: ½ vegetable

■ ■ ■

Mediterranean Green Beans

Net Carbs: 9 g

1 (16 ounce) package frozen cut green beans   **.5 kg**

1 onion, chopped

1 to 2 cloves garlic, finely minced

1 (14½ ounce) can diced tomatoes seasoned with
 Italian herbs or other seasoning of choice   **396 g**

1. Cook green beans according to package directions. Drain and set aside.

2. In sprayed skillet or saucepan, cook and stir onions and garlic over medium heat 5 to 6 minutes. Add a few drops water if needed.

3. Pour seasoned tomatoes into onion mixture. Simmer about 10 minutes.

4. Stir in green beans and season to taste with salt substitute and pepper. Simmer until beans heat through.

Yield: 6 to 8 servings   Serving size: ½ cup (120 ml)

Calories: 53   Protein: 2 g   Carbohydrate: 11 g
Fat: less than 1 g   Cholesterol: 0 mg   Sodium: 301 mg
Calcium: 58 mg   Fiber: 2 g   Sugars: 6 g
Sugar Alcohol: 0 g

Food Exchanges: 1 vegetable

According to new research, people with diabetes may be healthier if they eat more of their protein from vegetables, beans, and grains, rather than meats.

Seasoned-Stuffed Mushrooms

Net Carbs: 4 g

12 large mushrooms	
1 tablespoon reduced-fat cream cheese (Neufchatel)	**15 ml**
2 teaspoons dried herbs	**10 ml**
2 tablespoons plain or seasoned breadcrumbs	**30 ml**

1. Preheat oven to 350° (176° C).

2. Remove stems from mushrooms and chop finely. Place caps on large sprayed baking pan.

3. In sprayed skillet over medium heat, cook and stir chopped mushroom stems 2 to 3 minutes. Stir in cream cheese, herb and breadcrumbs and cook and stir 1 to 2 minutes. Season to taste with salt substitute and pepper.

4. Spoon cream cheese mixture evenly into mushroom caps. Coat with cooking spray. Cover baking pan with aluminum foil and bake about 15 minutes until caps are tender. Remove foil and bake 5 to 6 minutes longer or until tops brown.

Optional: Add 1 tablespoon (15 ml) finely chopped green onions with tops to mushroom stems before cooking in skillet to add more color.

Yield: 4 servings   Serving size: 3 mushrooms

Calories: 37   Protein: 3 g   Carbohydrate: 4 g
Fat: 2 g   Cholesterol: 3 mg   Sodium: 42 mg
Calcium: 8 mg   Fiber: less than 1 g   Sugars: 1 g
Sugar Alcohol: 0 g

Food Exchanges: 0

*Non-stick cooking spray and non-stick surface pans
should be used to brown or "fry" foods.*

Spicy Okra and Tomatoes

Net Carbs: 6 g

1 (16 ounce) package sliced frozen okra, slightly thawed	**.5 kg**
1 tablespoon canola, peanut or olive oil	**15 ml**
1 teaspoon salt-free Creole seasoning	**5 ml**
2 (16 ounce) cans no-salt diced tomatoes with liquid	**2 (.5 kg)**

1. In non-stick skillet over medium high heat, cook and stir okra until excess liquid evaporates. When okra starts to stick, add oil. Continue to cook and stir constantly until okra becomes crisp-tender.

2. Stir in seasoning and tomatoes and reduce heat to medium. Cook uncovered, stirring frequently, about 30 minutes.

Variation: To prepare with fresh okra, heat oil in skillet over medium high heat. Add okra and stir constantly until it is crisp-tender.

Yield: 8 servings   Serving size: ½ cup (120 ml)

Calories: 63   Protein: 2 g   Carbohydrate: 11 g
Fat: less than 1 g   Cholesterol: 0 mg   Sodium: 76 mg
Calcium: 81 mg   Fiber: 5 g   Sugars: 4 g
Sugar Alcohol: 0 g

Food Exchanges: 1 vegetable

*Salt substitutes made with potassium chloride
have 0 milligrams of sodium.*

Twice-Baked Potatoes

Net Carbs: 12 g

4 baking potatoes

1 (8 ounce) package reduced-fat
cream cheese (Neufchatel)   **227 g**

1 (8 ounce) carton light sour cream   **227 g**

Choice of garnish: bacon bits, shredded reduced-fat cheddar cheese, chopped
green onions with tops

1. Preheat oven to 400° (202° C).

2. On shallow baking sheet, arrange potatoes. Bake about 45 minutes or until potatoes are tender.

3. Cut potatoes in half lengthwise. Scoop out insides and leave shells intact.

4. In mixing bowl, mix potato with cream cheese and sour cream. Season to taste with salt substitute and pepper.

5. Mound potato filling in potato shells. Sprinkle each potato with choice of garnish.

6. Return potatoes to oven for 5 to 6 minutes and serve hot.

Yield: 8 servings   Serving size: 1 stuffed potato shell (½ potato)

Calories (without garnish): 149   Protein: 6 g   Carbohydrate: 12 g
Fat: 9 g   Cholesterol: 30 mg   Sodium: 133 mg
Calcium: 82 mg   Fiber: less than 1 g Sugars: 2 g
Sugar Alcohol: 0 g

Food Exchanges: 2 fat, ½ bread

A plain baked potato has about 160 calories and 0% fat.
Adding 2 teaspoons margarine and 2 tablespoons sour cream,
however, increases calories to 295 and fat to 46%!

❧ Cinnamon-Maple Sweet Potatoes

Net Carbs: 13 g

2 sweet potatoes	
2 teaspoons ground cinnamon	**10 ml**
1 tablespoon finely grated orange peel	**15 ml**
2 tablespoons sugar-free maple syrup	**30 ml**

1. Scrub sweet potatoes and prick skins. Cover and cook in microwave on HIGH for 4 minutes on each side or just until potatoes are soft. Let stand 1 to 2 minutes.

2. Scoop potato from shells and mash with fork. Into 3 to 4 small serving bowls, measure ⅓ cup (80 ml) potato. Sprinkle with cinnamon and orange peel and drizzle with syrup.

Yield: 3 to 4 servings   Serving size: ⅓ cup (80 ml)

Calories: 66   Protein: 1 g   Carbohydrate: 16 g
Fat: less than 1 g   Cholesterol: 0 mg   Sodium: 19 mg
Calcium: 41 mg   Fiber: 3 g   Sugars: 3 g
Sugar Alcohol: less than 1 g

Food Exchanges: 1 bread, ½ vegetable

■ ■ ■

Crunchy Potato Cakes

Net Carbs: 7 g

1 cup mashed potato flakes	240 ml
3 tablespoons light sour cream	45 ml
1 cup crushed bite-size crispy corn cereal squares	240 ml
2 teaspoons canola, peanut or olive oil	10 ml

1. Using 1¼ cups (300 ml) water (no milk or margarine), prepare 1 cup (240 ml) mashed potatoes according to package directions.

2. Mix sour cream with potatoes and season to taste with salt substitute and pepper.

3. For 1 potato cake, lightly pack potato mixture into ⅛ cup (30 ml) measuring cup (same size as a coffee measuring cup). Turn out onto palm and roll into 2-inch (5 cm) ball. Flatten into 3-inch (8 cm) cake. Repeat with remaining potato mixture.

4. Preheat non-stick skillet with ½ teaspoon (2 ml) oil over medium high heat. Coat 3 to 4 potato cakes on both sides with crushed cereal and place in hot skillet. Cook about 3 to 4 minutes on each side.

5. With spatula, remove potato cakes from pan and keep warm on baking sheet in 250° (121° C) oven. Do not cover or cakes will soften.

6. Repeat cooking process with remaining potato cakes. Add only ½ teaspoon (2 ml) oil as needed. Serve immediately.

Yield: About 8 servings   Serving size: 1 potato cake (1 ounce or ⅛ cup)
                                                    (28 g - 30 ml)

Calories: 46   Protein: 1 g   Carbohydrate: 7 g
Fat: 2 g   Cholesterol: 2 mg   Sodium: 28 mg
Calcium: 19 mg   Fiber: less than 1 g   Sugars: less than 1 g
Sugar Alcohol: 0 g

Food Exchanges: ½ bread, ½ fat

■ ■ ■

❧ Cheesy Squash Casserole

Net Carbs: 5 g

2 pounds yellow crookneck squash, thinly sliced	**1 kg**
¾ cup shredded reduced-fat sharp	
cheddar cheese, divided	**180 ml**
¼ cup light or fat-free mayonnaise	**60 ml**
¼ cup Egg Beaters® egg substitute	**60 ml**

1. In Dutch oven, cover squash with water and heat until water boils. Cook 8 to 10 minutes or just until squash is tender. Drain well in wire mesh strainer and gently press out liquid with fingers.

2. Preheat oven to 350° (176° C).

3. Return squash to Dutch oven, add ½ cup (120 ml) cheese, mayonnaise and egg substitute and mix well. Season to taste with salt substitute and pepper.

4. Spoon into sprayed 1½ to 2-quart (1 - 1.9 L) baking dish. Sprinkle with remaining ¼ cup (60 ml) cheese.

6. Bake uncovered about 30 minutes.

Yield: 9 servings (about 3 cups/710 ml)   Serving size: ½ cup (120 ml)

Calories: 106   Protein: 6 g   Carbohydrate: 6 g
Fat: 7 g   Cholesterol: 16 mg   Sodium: 213 mg
Calcium: 158 mg   Fiber: 1 g   Sugars: 2 g
Sugar Alcohol: 0 g

Food Exchanges: 1 fat, ½ vegetable

■ ■ ■

Italian-Herbed Tomato Halves

Net Carbs: 12 g

4 tomatoes, halved
3 tablespoons grated parmesan or romano cheese   **45 ml**
1 cup Italian-herb-seasoned breadcrumbs   **240 ml**

1. Preheat oven to 375° (190° C).

2. In shallow baking pan, arrange tomatoes.

3. In mixing bowl, combine cheese and crumbs and season to taste with salt
    substitute and pepper. Sprinkle crumb mixture over tomato halves.

4. Bake 15 to 20 minutes or until tomatoes heat through and topping browns.

Yield: 8 servings   Serving size: 1 tomato half

Calories: 74   Protein: 3 g   Carbohydrate: 13 g
Fat: 1 g   Cholesterol: 2 mg   Sodium: 429 mg
Calcium: 42 mg   Fiber: 1 g   Sugars: 2 g
Sugar Alcohol: 0

Food Exchanges: 1 bread

■ ■ ■

Creamy Mixed Vegetables

Net Carbs: 8 g

1 (16 ounce) frozen vegetable blend	
(such as broccoli, cauliflower, carrot blend)	**.5 kg**
1 tablespoon margarine or butter (not light)	**15 ml**
1 tablespoon all-purpose flour	**15 ml**
1¼ cups skim milk	**300 ml**

1. Cook vegetables according to package instructions. Drain and keep warm.

2. In saucepan over medium heat, melt margarine. Using wire whisk, stir in flour and cook about 2 minutes.

3. Add skim milk, cook and stir until sauce thickens. Season to taste with salt substitute and pepper.

4. Spoon sauce over vegetables to serve.

Optional: Add ½ cup (120 ml) reduced-fat shredded Swiss or cheddar cheese to thickened sauce.

Yield: 4 to 6 servings   Serving size: ½ cup (120 ml)

Calories: 75   Protein: 3 g   Carbohydrate: 10 g
Fat: 2 g   Cholesterol: 1 mg   Sodium: 76 mg
Calcium: 79 mg   Fiber: 2 g   Sugars: 5 g
Sugar Alcohol: 0 mg

Food Exchanges: ½ bread, ½ milk

Dark green and deep yellow vegetables such as spinach, broccoli, carrots and sweet potatoes have highest nutritional value.

Roasted Mixed Vegetables

Net Carbs: 3 g

2 pounds or more vegetables (asparagus, bell pepper, broccoli, eggplant, mushrooms, squash or onions)	**1 kg**
¼ cup canola, peanut or olive oil	**60 ml**
2 teaspoons crushed dried herbs (thyme, oregano, tarragon, rosemary or herb blend)	**10 ml**

1. Preheat oven to 400° (202° C).

2. Clean and trim vegetables. In large saucepan, heat 3 quarts (2.8 L) water until it boils. Blanch vegetables by adding to boiling water and cooking just until vegetables are barely tender.

3. Immediately immerse in cold water and drain on paper towels. Continue with remaining vegetables.

4. In roasting pan, lightly toss drained vegetables with oil. Roast in oven 5 to 6 minutes or until vegetables brown in spots.

5. Season to taste with salt substitute and pepper. Serve warm or at room temperature.

Yield: 8 to 10 servings   Serving size: ½ cup (120 ml)

Calories: 81	Protein: 3 g	Carbohydrate: 5 g
Fat: 6 g	Cholesterol: 0 mg	Sodium: 18 g
Calcium: 35 mg	Fiber: 2 g	Sugars: 2 g
Sugar Alcohol: 0 g		

Food Exchanges: 1 fat, ½ vegetable

■ ■ ■

Mushroom-Rice Pilaf

Net Carbs: 10 g

1 cup frozen seasoning blend	
(onions, celery, peppers, parsley)	**240 ml**
1 cup coarsely chopped fresh mushrooms	**240 ml**
1½ cups Swanson® Natural Goodness™ chicken broth	**360 ml**
½ cup uncooked brown rice	**120 ml**

1. To sprayed saucepan over medium heat, add frozen seasoning blend. Cook and stir until vegetables are tender. Add water if needed.

2. Add mushrooms, cook and stir about 2 minutes.

3. Gradually add chicken broth and heat until mixture boils. Stir in brown rice, black pepper and salt substitute to taste.

4. Reduce heat, cover and simmer about 50 minutes. Add more broth if needed.

Yield: 8 servings (About 3 cups/710 ml)

Serving size: About ⅓ cup (80 ml)

Calories: 54
Fat: less than 1 g
Calcium: 8 mg
Sugar Alcohol: 0 g

Protein: 2 g
Cholesterol: 0 mg
Fiber: less than 1 g

Carbohydrate: 10 g
Sodium: 109 mg
Sugars: less than 1 g

Food Exchanges: ½ bread

■ ■ ■

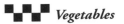

Creamy Broccoli and Noodles

Net Carbs: 13 g

1 (16 ounce) package frozen broccoli florets or chopped broccoli	.5 kg
1 (3 ounce) package chicken-flavored ramen noodles with flavor pack	84 g
1 (10¾ ounce) can Campbell's® Healthy Request® cream of mushroom condensed soup	280 g
½ cup sliced water chestnuts, drained, rinsed	120 ml

1. In large saucepan or Dutch oven, cook broccoli according to package instructions. Do not overcook. Drain and set aside.

2. In same saucepan, cook noodles according to package instructions and add flavor pack. Stir in broccoli, soup and water chestnuts.

Variation: Substitute 1 cup (240 ml) cooked cubed chicken for water chestnuts.

Yield: 6 to 8 servings (3 to 4 cups/710 g - .9 L)   Serving size: ½ cup (120 ml)

Calories: 102
Fat: 3 g
Calcium: 49 mg
Sugar Alcohol: 0 g

Protein: 3 g
Cholesterol: 2 mg
Fiber: 2 g

Carbohydrate: 15 g
Sodium: 368 mg
Sugars: 2 g

Food Exchanges: 1 bread, ½ vegetable, ½ fat

Stir pasta during the first 1 to 2 minutes of cooking to keep it from sticking.

Green Chili Cheese Casserole

Net Carbs: 8 g

1 (12 ounce) package reduced-carb spaghetti	340 g
1 (10 ounce) can mild green chili sauce	280 g
1 (10¾ ounce) can Campbell's® Healthy Request®	
cream of mushroom condensed soup	280 g
1½ to 2 cups shredded reduced-fat cheddar,	
jack or mozzarella cheese, divided	360 - 480 ml

1. In saucepan, cook spaghetti according to package directions.

2. Preheat oven to 350° (176° C).

3. Drain spaghetti and return to saucepan. Stir in green chili sauce, mushroom soup and 1 cup (240 ml) cheese.

4. Transfer spaghetti mixture to sprayed 9 x 13-inch (23 x 33 cm) baking dish. Sprinkle remaining ½ cup (120 ml) cheese on top.

5. Bake at 350° (176° C) for 25 to 30 minutes or until casserole bubbles and heats through.

Yield: 16 servings (about 8 cups/1.9 L)   Serving size: ½ cup (120 ml)

Calories (without Green Chile Sauce): 154 Protein: 11 g   Carbohydrate: 13 g
Fat: 6 g   Cholesterol: 16 mg   Sodium: 290 mg
Calcium: 167 mg   Fiber: 5 g   Sugars: less than 1 g
Sugar Alcohol: 0 mg

Food Exchanges: 1 bread, 1 low fat milk, 1 fat

■ ■ ■

Homemade Mac N Cheese

Net Carbs: 5 g

This is great served with 2 cups (480 ml) reduced-carb elbow, macaroni, penne or rigatoni pasta.

1 tablespoon regular margarine or butter (not light)	**15 ml**
1 tablespoon all-purpose flour	**15 ml**
1 cup skim milk	**240 ml**
4 ounces light processed cheese	**114 g**

1. In heavy saucepan over medium heat, melt margarine. Using wire whisk, stir in flour and cook for 1 minute.

2. Add milk all at once and cook and stir until mixture boils. Boil and stir 1 minute until sauce thickens and is smooth.

3. Remove sauce from heat, add cheese and stir until cheese melts. Season to taste with salt substitute and pepper. Serve with cooked pasta.

Yield: 6 servings   Serving size: ¼ cup (60 ml) sauce

Calories (sauce only): 75   Protein: 5 g   Carbohydrate: 5 g
Fat: 4 g   Cholesterol: 11 mg   Sodium: 340 mg
Calcium: 38 mg   Fiber: less than 1 g   Sugars: 3 g
Sugar Alcohol: 0 g

Food Exchanges: 1 fat, ½ low fat milk, ½ bread

Two ounces (57 g) dry pasta will make about 1 cup (240 ml) cooked pasta. Spaghetti and macaroni products usually double in volume when cooked. Egg noodles don't expand quite as much.

Green Chili Sauce

Net Carbs: 3 g

1 tablespoon margarine or butter (not light)	**15 ml**
1½ tablespoons flour	**22 ml**
1½ cups Swanson® Natural Goodness™ chicken broth	**360 ml**
1 (4 ounce) can mild diced green chilies with liquid	**114 g**

1. In heavy saucepan over medium heat, melt butter and stir in flour. When mixture bubbles, continue to cook and stir 1 minute.

2. Gradually stir in broth and heat until it boils. Cook and stir 1 minute.

3. Add green chilies and simmer 15 to 20 minutes.

4. Use immediately or cover and chill for later use.

Optional: Add ½ cup (120 ml) finely chopped onion and 1 finely minced garlic clove to butter before adding flour. Add pinch ground cumin.

Yield: 6 servings (1½ cups/360 ml)   Serving size: ¼ cup (60 ml)

Calories: 31	Protein: 1 g	Carbohydrate: 3 g
Fat: 2 g	Cholesterol: 0 mg	Sodium: 219 mg
Calcium: 16 mg	Fiber: less than 1 g	Sugars: less than 1 g
Sugar Alcohol: 0 g		

Food Exchanges: ½ fat

◆

Stock or broth is a strained, thin, clear liquid in which meat, poultry, or fish has been simmered with vegetables and herbs. Make your own or shop for reduced sodium, low fat canned broth.

Tex-Mex Black Bean Soup

Net Carbs: 12 g

⅓ cup finely chopped onion	80 ml
½ clove garlic, minced or pressed	
¼ teaspoon dried oregano leaves or ground cumin	2 ml
1 (15½ ounce) can black beans with liquid	425 g

1. Preheat sprayed large saucepan over medium heat. Add chopped onion and garlic and cook and stir 2 to 3 minutes. Stir in oregano and cook about 1 minute longer. Remove from heat.

2. In food processor or blender, process beans with liquid until desired consistency (chunky or smooth). For thinner soup, add small amount water.

3. Pour bean puree in saucepan with onion and garlic mixture. Heat until mixture boils, reduce heat and simmer 10 minutes for flavors to blend. Season to taste with salt substitute and pepper.

Yield: 4 servings   Serving size: ½ cup (120 ml)

Calories: 106	Protein: 7 g	Carbohydrate: 20 g
Fat: less than 1 g	Cholesterol: 0 mg	Sodium: 422 mg
Calcium: 44 mg	Fiber: 8 g	Sugars: less than 1 g
Sugar Alcohol: 0 g		

Food Exchanges: 1½ bread

Mince – cut into tiny, irregular pieces about 1/8 inch (.3 cm) in size.

Spicy Southwestern Soup

Net Carbs: 1 g

4 (14 ounce) cans Swanson® Natural Goodness™ chicken broth	4 (396 g)
1 (10 ounce) can mild diced tomatoes and green chilies with liquid	280 g
1 to 2 teaspoons chili powder	5 - 10 ml
½ teaspoon ground cumin	2 ml

1. In large saucepan or Dutch oven, combine all ingredients.

2. Simmer 30 minutes for flavors to blend.

Optional: Serve with No-Guilt Tortilla Crisps, (p. 24).

Yield: 8 servings
Calories: 10 g
Fat: less than 1 g
Calcium: 20 mg
Sugar Alcohol: 0 g
Food Exchanges: 0

Serving size: 1 cup (240 ml)
Protein: 1 g
Cholesterol: 0 mg
Fiber: less than 1 g

Carbohydrate: 1 g
Sodium: 204 mg
Sugars: less than 1 g

Emergency Chicken-Noodle Soup

Net Carbs: 9 g

1 (3 ounce) package chicken-flavored ramen noodles and flavor pack	84 g
2 (14 ounce) cans Swanson® Natural Goodness™ chicken broth	2 (396 g)
1 cup frozen peas and carrots or mixed vegetables	240 ml
1 cup cubed cooked chicken breasts	240 ml

1. Prepare noodles according to package directions and set aside.

2. In large saucepan, heat chicken broth until it boils. Add vegetables and cook 4 to 5 minutes. Add chicken and noodles and season to taste with salt substitute and black pepper.

Yield: 8 servings
Calories: 94
Fat: 3 g
Calcium: 7 mg
Sugar Alcohol: 0 g
Food Exchanges: ½ bread, ½ fat

Serving size: 1 cup (240 ml)
Protein: 8 g
Cholesterol: 15 mg
Fiber: less than 1 g

Carbohydrate: 9 g
Sodium: 438 mg
Sugars: 1 g

Vegetable Soup with Herbs

Net Carbs: 8 g

3 (14 ounce) cans Swanson® Natural Goodness™
   chicken broth   **396 g**
Soup Herb Blend (below) or other salt-free seasoning blend to taste
1 (16 ounce) package frozen vegetables for soup mix
   (tomatoes, potatoes, corn, carrots, butter beans, okra,
   green beans, onions, celery)   **.5 kg**

1. In large pot, pour broth and heat until it boils.

2. Stir in Soup Herb Blend and frozen vegetables. Reduce heat and simmer 15 to 20 minutes.

3. Remove bay leaf and serve hot.

Optional: Add ⅛ teaspoon (.5 ml) garlic powder with herbs.

Yield: 6 servings (6 cups/1.5 L) Serving size: 1 cup (240 ml)
Calories: 45   Protein: 3 g   Carbohydrate: 8 g
Fat: 0 g   Cholesterol: 0 mg   Sodium: 508 mg
Calcium: 0 mg   Fiber: less than 1 g   Sugars: 3 g
Sugar Alcohol: 0 g
Food Exchanges: ½ vegetable

Soup Herb-Blend

Use this salt-free seasoning to flavor your favorite soups.

2 small or 1 large bay leaf
1 teaspoon crushed dried basil   **5 ml**
¼ teaspoon crushed dried thyme   **1 ml**
8 whole peppercorns

1. Combine ingredients and add to boiling or simmering soup for hearty flavors. Remove bay leaf and any visible peppercorns when soup is ready to serve.

*Optional: Add ⅛ teaspoon (.5 ml) garlic powder or 1 fresh garlic clove, minced.
        Tie herbs in cheesecloth bag or place in metal tea ball before adding to
        soup.*

Main Dishes

No-Beans Chili

Net Carbs: 5 g

1 onion, finely chopped	
1 (1 pound) package lean ground beef	**.5 kg**
1 (10 ounce) can mild diced	
tomatoes and green chilies	**280 g**
1 (1.25 ounce) packet reduced-sodium	
taco seasoning mix	**36 g**

1. In sprayed large skillet over medium heat, cook and stir onion until tender. Do not brown. Remove and set aside.

2. In same skillet over medium heat, cook and stir ground beef until it browns. Transfer to wire mesh strainer and drain. Wipe skillet with paper towels to remove excess fat.

3. Return meat and onion to skillet. Stir in tomatoes, taco seasoning and 1 to 2 cups (240 - 480 ml) water. Simmer 25 to 30 minutes for flavors to blend.

Optional: Serve with No-Guilt Tortilla Crisps, (p. 24).

Yield: 8 servings   Serving size: ½ cup (120 ml)

Calories: 131   Protein: 13 g   Carbohydrate: 5 g
Fat: 6 g   Cholesterol: 36 g   Sodium: 366 mg
Calcium: 23 mg   Fiber: less than 1 g   Sugars: 3 g
Sugar Alcohol: 0 g

Food Exchanges: 1½ medium fat meat, ½ other carb, ½ vegetable

Chop – cut into small, irregular pieces about 1⁄4 inch (.6 cm) in size.

✄ Oven-Barbecued Brisket

Net Carbs: 1 g

3 pounds lean brisket, trimmed	1. 5 kg
1½ to 2 tablespoons Mrs. Dash® salt-free blend	
or Steak Grilling Blend™	20 - 30 ml
1 cup Carb Options™ barbecue sauce	240 ml

1. Preheat oven to 275° (135° C).

2. On large piece heavy duty, wide aluminum foil, place brisket and sprinkle generously on both sides with seasoning blend.

3. Seal brisket tightly in foil. Bake 2½ hours (or 1 hour per pound/.5 kg) and remove from oven to check for tenderness. When brisket is fork-tender, drain meat juices and reserve. Brush 1 cup (240 ml) barbecue sauce on brisket. Continue cooking for 20 to 30 minutes.

4. Remove brisket from oven. Transfer to baking pan or dish, seal tightly and chill. Pour reserved meat juices in separate container and chill. After juices cool, remove any congealed fat.

5. To prepare for serving, slice cold brisket across grain of meat. Lay slices in 9 x 13-inch (23 x 33 cm) or smaller baking dish. Pour reserved liquid over brisket.

6. Heat at 300° (148° C) until meat heats through.

Tip: Be sure to trim all visible fat from brisket.

Yield: 20 servings   Serving size: 1 slice (3 ounces/84 g) brisket

Calories: 149	Protein: 22 g	Carbohydrate: 1 g
Fat: 5 g	Cholesterol: 27 mg	Sodium: 167 mg
Calcium: 13 mg	Fiber: 0 g	Sugars: 0 g
Sugar Alcohol: 0 g		

Food Exchanges: 3 lean meat

To reduce fat in recipes, ALWAYS trim visible fat and skin BEFORE and AFTER cooking.

Quick and Easy
Beef-Stuffed Peppers

Net Carbs: 6 g

3 large green bell peppers, whole

1 onion, finely chopped

1 (1 pound) package lean ground beef   **.5 kg**

2 cups Carb Options™ garden-style sauce   **480 ml**

1. Cut peppers lengthwise into 2 halves. Remove stems, seeds and white membrane.

2. In medium saucepan, heat about 4 cups (.9 L) water until it boils. Drop peppers into boiling water and boil 5 to 6 minutes or until peppers are crisp tender. Plunge into cold water and set upside down on paper towels to drain.

3. Preheat oven to 350° (176° C).

4. In sprayed nonstick skillet over medium heat, cook and stir onion until tender. Remove from skillet and set aside.

5. Add ground beef to skillet, cook and stir until it browns. Drain meat in wire mesh strainer and wipe skillet with paper towels to remove any accumulated fat.

6. In skillet, combine ground beef, onion and 1 cup (240 ml) sauce. Mound mixture into peppers. Bake covered 20 minutes. Remove cover.

7. While peppers bake, heat remaining sauce in small saucepan.

8. Spoon sauce over baked peppers and serve immediately.

Variation: Substitute 2 cups (480 ml) no-salt tomato sauce for pasta sauce.

Yield: 6 servings   Serving size: 1 stuffed pepper half with sauce

Calories: 247   Protein: 16 g   Carbohydrate: 9 g
Fat: 16 g   Cholesterol: 52 mg   Sodium: 412 mg
Calcium: 16 mg   Fiber: 3 g   Sugars: 5 g
Sugar Alcohol: 0 g

Food Exchanges: 2 fat, ½ medium fat meat, ½ vegetable

Spaghetti Meat Sauce

Net Carbs: 4 g

½ (1 pound) package lean ground beef	227 g
½ (1 pound) package ground turkey	227 g
1 (1 pound 10 ounce) jar Carb Options™	
garden-style sauce	737 g
1 to 2 teaspoons dried basil or oregano	5 - 10 ml

1. In sprayed large skillet over medium heat, cook meat until it browns. Drain in wire mesh strainer. Wipe skillet with paper towels to remove any accumulated fat.

2. Return meat to skillet and add sauce, herbs and 1 cup (240 ml) water and mix well. Cover and simmer 30 minutes to allow flavors to blend.

Optional: Try Mrs. Dash® Salt-Free Classic Italian Seasoning Blend instead of basil or oregano for a little different flavor.

Yield: 8 servings   Serving size: ½ cup (120 ml)

Calories: 166   Protein: 12 g   Carbohydrate: 5 g
Fat: 10 g   Cholesterol: 42 mg   Sodium: 437 mg
Calcium: 7 mg   Fiber: 1 g   Sugars: 3 g
Sugar Alcohol: 0 g

Food Exchanges: 1½ medium fat meat, ½ vegetable

"Hamburger" meat may have added seasonings, fillers or fat—so choose clearly labeled "lean ground beef."

❧ Spicy Beef Enchiladas

Net Carbs: 11 g

¾ (1 pound) package lean ground beef or turkey breast	340 g
2 (10 ounce) cans mild red chili enchilada sauce, divided	2 (280 g)
8 (8 inch) low-carb tortillas	8 (20 cm)
1½ cups reduced-fat shredded cheddar, jack or mozzarella cheese	360 ml

1. Preheat oven to 375° (190° C).

2. In skillet over medium heat, cook and stir ground beef until it browns. Drain meat in wire mesh strainer to remove fat. Wipe skillet with paper towels to remove any accumulated fat. Reduce heat to low, return meat to skillet and mix with 1 can enchilada sauce. Cook and stir over low heat until sauce mixes well.

3. Spoon about 2 tablespoons (30 ml) meat mixture near edge of each tortilla. Add 1 to 2 tablespoons (15 - 30 ml) cheese, then roll tortilla and place seam side down in sprayed 11 x 7-inch (28 x 18 cm) or 9 x 9-inch (23 x 23 cm) baking dish. (If tortillas do not roll easily, heat between damp paper towels 10 to 15 seconds on HIGH power in microwave.)

4. Coat rolled tortillas with cooking spray. Bake 15 minutes.

5. While enchiladas are baking, heat half remaining can enchilada sauce in saucepan. Store remaining sauce for later use.

6. Remove enchiladas from oven and spread with hot enchilada sauce. Top with remaining cheese. Return to oven 5 to 10 minutes or until cheese melts. Serve immediately.

Optional: If you want to make your own enchilada sauce, try Red Chili Enchilada Sauce on page 140.

Yield: 8 enchiladas   Serving size: 1 enchilada

Calories (with sauce): 369   Protein: 25 g   Carbohydrate: 24 g
Fat: 20 g   Cholesterol: 58 mg   Sodium: 694 mg
Calcium: 337 mg   Fiber: 13 g   Sugars: 5 g
Sugar Alcohol: 0 g

Food Exchanges: 2½ medium fat meat, 1 bread, 1 fat, ½ vegetable

Stir-Fry Steak and Bok Choy

Net Carbs: 1 g

½ **pound lean boneless flank or top sirloin steak,**	
trimmed	**227 g**
1 head bok choy	
3 teaspoons canola, peanut or olive oil	**15 ml**
1 cup Stir-Fry Cooking Sauce (p. 143)	**240 ml**

1. Slice steak into 1 x 3-inch (2.5 x 8 cm) thin strips and set aside.

2. Wash bok choy carefully and cut leaves from stems. Cut stems in ¼-inch (.6 cm) slices and shred leaves.

3. Heat non-stick surface wok or large skillet over high heat. Add 1 teaspoon (5 ml) oil and bok choy stems. Cook uncovered, stirring constantly, 1 to 2 minutes.

4. Add ¼ cup (60 ml) water, cover and cook additional 2 minutes. Add leaves and cook and stir 1 to 2 more minutes. Remove bok choy from wok.

5. Pour remaining 2 teaspoons (10 ml) oil into wok. When oil is hot, add steak. Cook and stir until meat browns slightly, about 3 to 4 minutes.

6. Stir in Stir-Fry Cooking Sauce and return bok choy to wok. Cook and stir until sauce boils and thickens.

Yield: 4 servings   Serving size: 1 cup (240 ml)

Calories (without sauce): 137   Protein: 14 g   Carbohydrate: 2 g
Fat: 8 g   Cholesterol: 24 mg   Sodium: 65 mg
Calcium: 101 mg   Fiber: 1 g   Sugars: less than 1 g
Sugar Alcohol: 0 g

Food Exchanges: 1 fat, ½ medium fat meat

Mama's Meat Loaf

Net Carbs: 9 g

1 (14½ ounce) can stewed tomatoes with Mexican flavors (jalapeno, garlic and cumin), divided	396 g
1 (1 pound) package lean ground beef or turkey breast	.5 kg
½ cup Egg Beaters® egg substitute	120 ml
1 cup old-fashion rolled oats, uncooked	240 ml

1. Preheat oven to 350° (176° C).

2. In food processor or blender, process tomatoes about 5 to 10 seconds. In mixing bowl, combine all ingredients and season to taste with salt substitute and pepper.

3. Pack meat mixture in sprayed 9 x 5 x 3-inch (23 x 13 x 8 cm) loaf pan.

4. Bake about 1½ hours or until meat cooks. Drain fat from loaf pan 1 to 2 times during cooking.

Yield: About 6 servings   Serving size: 1 (1 inch/2.5 cm) slice

Calories: 215   Protein: 17 g   Carbohydrate: 9 g
Fat: 12 g   Cholesterol: 51 mg   Sodium: 410 mg
Calcium: 53 mg   Fiber: less than 1 g   Sugars: 4 g
Sugar Alcohol: 0 g

Food Exchanges: 2 medium fat meat, 1 bread, ½ fat, ½ vegetable

■ ■ ■

Beef-Stuffed Cabbage Rolls

Net Carbs: 5 g

1 (2½ pound) large head cabbage	1.2 kg
1 (16 ounce) package frozen seasoning blend	
(onions, celery, peppers, parsley), slightly thawed	.5 kg
1 (1 pound) package lean ground beef or	
ground turkey breast	.5 kg
¼ cup Egg Beaters® egg substitute	60 ml

1. Remove 10 to 12 large leaves from cabbage. Trim thick rib from back of each leaf to be even with rest of leaf. Immerse leaves in boiling water 5 to 6 minutes or until thick part is crisp-tender. Remove and drain.

2. In sprayed skillet over medium heat, cook and stir seasoning blend until liquid evaporates and vegetables are tender. Remove from skillet and set aside.

3. Add ground beef to skillet and cook and stir until meat browns. Drain meat in wire mesh strainer.

4. Wipe skillet with paper towels and return seasoning blend and meat to skillet. Season to taste with salt substitute and pepper. Stir in egg substitute.

5. Place 1 to 2 tablespoons (15 - 30 ml) meat mixture near end of each cabbage leaf. Roll leaves to enclose meat mixture and tuck ends under.

6. In steamer basket in large pot or electric steamer, arrange 1 layer cabbage rolls. Steam each batch 15 to 20 minutes or until cabbage is tender.

Optional: Serve with Mustard Sauce (p. 143).

Yield: 10 to 12 servings   Serving size: 1 cabbage roll

Calories: 122   Protein: 11 g   Carbohydrate: 8 g
Fat: 5 g   Cholesterol: 29 mg   Sodium: 67 mg
Calcium: 53 mg   Fiber: 3 g   Sugars: 5 g
Sugar Alcohol: 0 g

Food Exchanges: ½ medium fat meat, ½ vegetable, ½ fat

■ ■ ■

Wild Rice-Stuffed Cabbage Rolls

Net Carbs: 19 g

8 large cabbage leaves	
1 (6 ounce) package reduced-sodium	
long grain and wild rice mix	**168 g**
1 cup reduced-fat shredded Swiss or	
jack cheese, divided	**240 ml**
1 (4 ounce) can no-salt tomato sauce	**114 g**

1. Cook rice according to package directions. While rice is cooking, prepare cabbage leaves.

2. Trim rib from the back of each cabbage leaf to be even with the rest of the leaf. In saucepan, heat water until it boils. Immerse cabbage leaves in boiling water 5 to 6 minutes or until leaves wilt. Drain.

3. In mixing bowl, combine ¾ cup (180 ml) cheese and 1½ cups (360 ml) cooked rice (reserve remaining rice for later use).

4. Spoon 2 to 3 tablespoons (30 - 45 ml) rice mixture onto cabbage leaf. Roll sides of leaf over rice mixture, then fold in both ends of leaf.

5. In steamer basket in large pot or electric steamer, place rolls seam side down and steam 30 to 35 minutes or until cabbage is tender.

6. Heat tomato sauce and season to taste with salt substitute and pepper. Pour over cooked cabbage rolls and sprinkle with remaining ¼ cup (60 ml) cheese. Let stand until cheese melts.

Variation: Instead of steaming cabbage rolls, pour tomato sauce over rolls and bake at 350° (176° C) for 35 to 40 minutes or until cabbage is tender. Remove from oven and sprinkle cheese on top.

Yield: 8 servings   Serving size: 1 cabbage roll with sauce

Calories: 221	Protein: 13 g	Carbohydrate: 20 g
Fat: 9 g	Cholesterol: 25 mg	Sodium: 346 mg
Calcium: 368 mg	Fiber: 1 g	Sugars: 2 g
Sugar Alcohol: 0 g		

Food Exchanges: 1 bread, 1 medium fat meat, ½ vegetable, ½ fat

■ ■ ■

❧ Grilled Pork Chops with Apples

Net Carbs: 0 g

4 (3 x 4 inch) boneless pork chops	**4 (8 x 10 cm)**
½ teaspoon Mrs. Dash® Chicken Grilling Blend™	**2 ml**
Maple Syrup Stir-Fry Apples (p. 149)	

1. Sprinkle pork chops with seasoning. Using outdoor grill, grill pork chops covered at 350° (176° C) to 400° (202° C) for about 10 minutes on each side. (To cook indoors, broil uncovered in oven about 10 minutes on each side.) Top pork chops with Maple Syrup Stir-Fry Apples.

Yield: 4 servings   Serving size: 1 boneless pork chop

Calories (without apples): 169   Protein: 25 g   Carbohydrate: 0 g
Fat: 7 g   Cholesterol: 62 mg   Sodium: 41 mg
Calcium: 5 mg   Fiber: 0 g   Sugars: 0 g
Sugar Alcohol: 0 g
Food Exchanges: 3½ lean meat

■ ■ ■

No-Fuss Pork Chop Packets

Net Carbs: 7 g

4 small boneless pork chops, trimmed	
1 teaspoon garlic powder	**5 ml**
1 white or yellow onion, sliced	
1 red or green apple, unpeeled, cored, cut in thick wedges	

1. Preheat oven to 325° (162° C). On each of 4 large (18 inch/45 cm) pieces aluminum foil, place 1 pork chop. Sprinkle with ¼ teaspoon (1 ml) garlic powder, salt substitute and pepper to taste. Add sliced onions and apple wedges. Seal pork chops tightly. Bake for 1 hour or until pork chops are tender.

Tip: Be sure to use garlic powder, not garlic salt.

Yield: 4 servings   Serving size: 1 pork chop pouch

Calories: 240   Protein: 23 g   Carbohydrate: 8 g
Fat: 13 g   Cholesterol: 66 mg   Sodium: 51 mg
Calcium: 31 mg   Fiber: 1 g   Sugars: 5 g
Sugar Alcohol: 0 g
Food Exchanges: 3 medium fat meat, 1 fruit, ½ vegetable

Fancy Grilled Ham and Cheese

Net Carbs: 13 g

2 slices low-carb whole wheat bread
2 to 3 teaspoons brown or dijon-style mustard   **10 - 15 ml**
2 slices 98% fat-free deli ham
1 slice fat free swiss cheese

1. Preheat skillet over medium heat.

2. Spread mustard on one slice bread and add ham and cheese.

3. Spray one side of sandwich with cooking spray and cook that side in skillet until it browns.

4. Spray other side with cooking spray and cook until it browns.

5. Serve warm.

Optional: Serve with 1 large dill pickle.

Yield: 1 serving

Calories: 155	Protein: 22 g	Carbohydrate: 17 g
Fat: 3 g	Cholesterol: 12 mg	Sodium: 825 mg
Calcium: 6 mg	Fiber: 4 g	Sugars: 3 g
Sugar Alcohol: 0 g		

Food Exchanges: 3 very lean meat, 1 bread

■ ■ ■

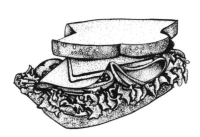

Hot Dog Wraps
Net Carbs: 14 g

4 (8 to 10 inch) low-carb or whole wheat tortillas   4 (20 - 25 cm)

4 regular size fat-free frankfurters

4 mozzarella string cheese sticks, pulled apart

Your choice of condiments (pickle relish, mustard, sugar-free ketchup)

1. Preheat oven to 375° (190° C).

2. Spray one side of tortillas with cooking spray and place a hot dog about 1 inch (2.5 cm) from edge of each.

3. Split hot dog down middle and insert cheese. Add condiments. Roll up hot dog inside tortilla.

4. In sprayed baking dish, place tortilla wraps seam side down. Coat each wrap with cooking spray.

5. Bake 10 to 15 minutes or until hot dog heats and cheese melts. If tortillas begin to dry out, remove from oven and spray with cooking spray, then return to oven.

Yield: 4 servings   Serving size: 1 hot dog wrap

Calories: 231	Protein: 18 g	Carbohydrate: 25 g
Fat: 7 g	Cholesterol: 28 mg	Sodium: 993 mg
Calcium: 219 mg	Fiber: 11 g	Sugars: 2 g
Sugar Alcohol: 0 g		

Food Exchanges: 1½ bread, 1 fat, ½ lean meat

■ ■ ■

Lemon-Garlic Baked Chicken

Net Carbs: less than 1 g

1 tablespoon fresh lemon juice	15 ml
1 tablespoon canola, peanut or olive oil	15 ml
1 clove garlic, finely minced	
1 (2½ to 3 pound) whole chicken,	
cut into serving pieces	1.2 - 1.5 kg

1. Preheat oven to 350° (176° C). In small bowl, combine lemon juice, oil, garlic and salt substitute and pepper to taste.

2. In shallow baking dish, arrange chicken in single layer. Pour lemon juice mixture over chicken.

3. Cover and bake, basting occasionally, about 45 minutes or until chicken is tender and juices run clear.

Yield: 6 to 8 servings
Calories: 134
Fat: 9 g
Calcium: 4 mg
Sugar Alcohol: 0 g

Serving size: 1 to 2 pieces chicken
Protein: 13 g   Carbohydrate: less than 1 g
Cholesterol: 46 mg Sodium: 135 mg
Fiber: less than 1 g Sugars: less than 1 g
Food Exchanges: 1 medium fat meat, ½ fat

■ ■ ■

Curried Chicken

Net Carbs: 5 g

1 (10¾ ounce) can Campbell's® Healthy Request® cream	
of mushroom condensed soup	280 g
1 teaspoon curry powder	5 ml
4 boneless, skinless chicken breast halves, cooked, cubed	
⅓ cup slivered almonds, toasted	80 ml

1. In large saucepan, combine soup, ½ soup can water and curry. Stir in cubed chicken. Heat and stir until mixture heats through. Sprinkle with almonds just before serving.

Yield: 6 servings
Calories: 185
Fat: 7 g
Calcium: 59 mg
Sugar Alcohol: 0 g

Serving size: ⅔ cup (160 ml)
Protein: 25 g   Carbohydrate: 6 g
Cholesterol: 59 mg Sodium: 455 mg
Fiber: 1 g   Sugars: 1 g
Food Exchanges: 1 lean meat, ½ other carb, ½ fat

"Fried" Chicken

Net Carbs: 16 g

1 cup skim milk	**240 ml**
4 boneless, skinless chicken breast halves	
1 to 1½ cups whole grain or	
whole wheat Melba toast crumbs	**240 - 360 ml**
1 teaspoon dried herbs or Mrs. Dash®	
salt-free seasoning blend of your choice	**5 ml**

1. In container with lid, soak chicken breasts in milk. Cover and chill about 30 minutes.

2. Preheat oven to 375° (190° C).

3. Mix toast crumbs and seasoning. Drain chicken breasts and coat with crumbs, pressing crumbs lightly on both sides of chicken with fingers.

4. On lightly sprayed baking sheet, place chicken. Bake 20 minutes and check for doneness by piercing chicken with knife. Chicken is done when meat is tender and juices run clear.

Yield: 4 servings   Serving size: 1 chicken breast

Calories: 261   Protein: 38 g   Carbohydrate: 17 g
Fat: 4 g   Cholesterol: 86 mg   Sodium: 594 mg
Calcium: 64 mg   Fiber: 1 g   Sugars: 3 g
Sugar Alcohol: 0 g   Food Exchanges: 4½ very lean meat, 1 bread, ½ milk

■ ■ ■

Citrus-Baked Chicken

Net Carbs: less than 1 g

1 lime

⅓ cup lite (reduced sodium) soy sauce   **80 ml**

½ teaspoon ground ginger   **2 ml**

4 small boneless, skinless chicken breast halves

1. Finely grate ½ teaspoon (2 ml) lime peel and squeeze 1 tablespoon (15 ml) lime juice.

2. In small saucepan, combine soy sauce, lime peel and juice, ginger and 3 tablespoons (45 ml) water. Heat mixture until it boils and boil 1 minute. Cool to room temperature.

3. In resealable plastic bag or container, place chicken breasts and pour cooled marinade over chicken. Refrigerate several hours or overnight.

4. Preheat oven to 350° (176° C).

5. Pour off marinade. In sprayed baking dish, bake chicken covered about 45 minutes or until chicken is tender and juices run clear.

6. Uncover and brown chicken breasts under oven broiler 5 minutes on each side.

Yield: 4 servings   Serving size: 1 chicken breast half

Calories: 190   Protein: 35 g   Carbohydrate: less than 1 g
Fat: 4 g   Cholesterol: 96 mg   Sodium: 228 mg
Calcium: 20 mg   Fiber: less than 1 g   Sugars: less than 1 g
Sugar Alcohol: 0 g

Food Exchanges: 5 very lean meat

◆

*Four ounces (115 g) raw meat is equal to 3 ounces
(85 g) cooked meat, or 3 meat exchanges. Weigh meat
portions after cooking and removing bones and fat.*

❧ Ultimate Broccoli-Cheese Chicken

Net Carbs: 5 g

¼ cup pine nuts or slivered almonds	60 ml
2 (10 ounce) packages frozen broccoli florets in cheese sauce	2 (280 g)
3 cups cubed cooked chicken or turkey breasts	710 ml
¼ cup diced pimentos	60 ml

1. In dry skillet over medium heat, cook and stir nuts until they brown.

2. Cook frozen broccoli in sauce according to package directions.

3. Transfer to large saucepan and stir in chicken and pimentos.

4. Simmer, stirring constantly, until chicken and broccoli mixture heats through. Add water if necessary to thin sauce. Season to taste with salt substitute and pepper. Remove from heat and keep warm.

5. Sprinkle mixture with toasted nuts just before serving.

Yield: 6 to 8 servings   Serving size: ⅔ cup (160 ml)

Calories: 244   Protein: 34 g   Carbohydrate: 7 g
Fat: 9 g   Cholesterol: 84 mg   Sodium: 448 mg
Calcium: 59 mg   Fiber: 2 g   Sugars: 4 g
Sugar Alcohol: 0 g

Food Exchanges: 1½ lean meat, ½ vegetable, ½ fat

■ ■ ■

Chicken-Mushroom Oven Packets

Net Carbs: 5 g

1 cup sliced fresh mushrooms, divided	240 ml
1 sliced yellow or white onion, divided	
4 small boneless, skinless chicken breast halves	
8 tablespoons Carb Options™ olive oil vinaigrette dressing	120 ml

1. Preheat oven to 350° (176° C).

2. On each of 4 (18 inch/45 cm) pieces aluminum foil, place mushrooms, onions and then chicken breasts. Season chicken with salt substitute and pepper.

3. Fold up sides of foil and spoon 2 tablespoons (30 ml) dressing into each packet.

4. Seal packet tightly and bake 30 minutes. Open packet and baste chicken and vegetables with dressing. Reseal packet and continue baking for additional 30 minutes.

5. Serve in packet or remove to serving plate.

Yield: 4 servings   Serving size: 1 chicken breast and vegetables

Calories: 253   Protein: 37 g   Carbohydrate: 5 g
Fat: 11 g   Cholesterol: 85 mg   Sodium: 644 mg
Calcium: 9 mg   Fiber: less than 1 g   Sugars: 3 g
Sugar Alcohol: 0 g

Food Exchanges: 5 lean meat, ½ vegetable

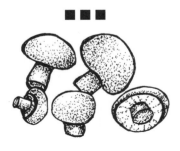

Teriyaki Chicken Tenders

Net Carbs: 9 g

1 pound boneless, skinless chicken tenders	**.5 kg**
⅓ cup plus 2 teaspoons Carb Options™	
Asian teriyaki marinade, divided	**80 ml + 10 ml**
¼ cup sliced green onions with tops	**60 ml**
1 (8 ounce) can pineapple chunks or tidbits,	
juice reserved	**227 g**

1. In resealable plastic bag, place tenders and marinade. Refrigerate and marinate 15 to 20 minutes.

2. Preheat sprayed non-stick wok or skillet over high heat. Add about ½ chicken tenders and stir-fry 2 minutes or until chicken browns. Remove first batch cooked chicken and keep warm. Repeat with remaining chicken.

3. Add green onions, pineapple with 1 tablespoon (15 ml) pineapple juice and 1 to 2 teaspoons (5 - 10 ml) marinade to wok and cook and stir about 1 minute.

4. Spoon onions and pineapple over chicken tenders and serve immediately.

Variation: Substitute 1 pound (.5 kg) cubed lean boneless pork for chicken tenders.

Yield: 4 servings   Serving size: 2 chicken tenders

Calories: 141   Protein: 22   Carbohydrate: 9 g
Fat: 6 g   Cholesterol: 66 mg   Sodium: 688 mg
Calcium: 5 mg   Fiber: less than 1 g Sugars: 7 g
Sugar Alcohol: 0 mg

Food Exchanges: 3 lean meat, ½ fruit

■ ■ ■

Cheesy Chicken Spaghetti

Net Carbs: 12 g

1 (12 ounce) package low-carb spaghetti	340 g
1 (16 ounce) package light processed cheese, cubed, divided	.5 kg
½ cup diced tomatoes and green chilies, drained, reserve liquid	120 ml
2 cups cubed cooked chicken	480 ml

1. In saucepan, prepare spaghetti according to package directions. Drain and return to saucepan.

2. Preheat oven to 350° (176° C).

3. Set aside ¼ cup (60 ml) cheese. In microwave-safe dish, mix remaining cheese and tomatoes and green chilies and cover. Heat mixture on HIGH for 1½ minutes. Remove, stir and return to microwave for additional 1½ minutes. Stir and let stand.

4. Combine cheese mixture with cooked spaghetti and chicken. If needed, add 1 tablespoon (15 ml) reserved tomato liquid.

5. Transfer to 9 x 13-inch (23 x 33 cm) baking dish and top with reserved cheese.

6. Bake, covered, about 25 to 30 minutes or until mixture bubbles and heats through.

Yield: 12 to 14 servings   Serving size: ½ cup (120 ml)

Calories: 202	Protein: 20 g	Carbohydrate: 18 g
Fat: 4 g	Cholesterol: 37 mg	Sodium: 660 mg
Calcium: 4 mg	Fiber: 6 g	Sugars: 3 g
Sugar Alcohol: 0 g		

Food Exchanges: 2 lean meat, 1 bread, 1 other carb

❧ Chicken and Dumplings

Net Carbs: 4 g

¼ cup plus 3 tablespoons reduced-fat baking mix	60 ml + 45 ml
¼ teaspoon crushed dried thyme	1 ml
2 (14 ounce) cans Swanson® Natural Goodness™ chicken broth	2 (396 g)
1 (12½ ounce) can 98% fat-free premium chicken breast in water or 2 cups (480 ml) cooked cubed chicken breasts	340 g

1. Stir baking mix and 3 tablespoons (45 ml) water to make soft dough. Add small amount baking mix if dough is too sticky. Add thyme, salt substitute and pepper to taste.

2. In medium saucepan over high heat, combine broth and chicken and heat until mixture boils. Drop dumpling mixture by tablespoonfuls onto boiling broth.

3. Reduce heat to medium (slow boil, not a simmer) and cook uncovered 10 minutes. Cover and continue cooking 10 more minutes.

4. Ladle into small bowls to serve.

Tip: Use the reduced-fat baking mix for biscuits, pancakes, dumplings.

Yield: About 6 servings (6 small dumplings plus chicken and broth)
Serving size: ½ to ¾ cup/120 - 180 ml (1 dumpling plus chicken and broth)

Calories: 77	Protein: 11 g	Carbohydrate: 4 g
Fat: 1 g	Cholesterol: 21 mg	Sodium: 554 mg
Calcium: 0 g	Fiber: 0 g	Sugars: less than 1 g
Sugar Alcohol: 0 g		

Food Exchanges: 1½ very lean meat

■ ■ ■

Chicken Italiano

Net Carb: 7 g

4 boneless, skinless chicken breast halves, rinsed, patted dry

¼ cup fat-free or light mayonnaise	**60 ml**
¼ cup Italian seasoned breadcrumbs	**60 ml**
¼ cup grated parmesan or romano cheese	**60 ml**

1. Preheat oven to 375° (190° C). Lightly spread mayonnaise on both sides of each chicken breast. In flat dish, mix breadcrumbs and cheese. Add salt substitute and pepper to taste.

2. Coat chicken with crumb mixture and transfer to baking sheet. (Cover baking sheet with aluminum foil for easier cleaning.) Bake 45 minutes or until chicken is tender and juices run clear.

Yield: 4 servings
Calories: 269
Fat: 10 g
Calcium: 65 mg
Sugar Alcohol: 0 g

Serving size: 1 chicken breast half
Protein: 37 g   Carbohydrate: 7 g
Cholesterol: 94 mg   Sodium: 684 mg
Fiber: less than 1 g   Sugars: 1 g
Food Exchanges: 1½ lean meat, 1 fat, ½ bread

■ ■ ■

Chicken and Wild Rice Supreme

Net Carbs: 21 g

1 (6 ounce) package reduced-sodium long grain and wild rice mix	**168 g**
2 boneless, skinless chicken breasts, cooked, cubed	
1 (10¾ ounce) can Campbell's® Healthy Request® cream of mushroom condensed soup	**280 g**
1 (4 ounce) jar diced pimentos with liquid	**114 g**

1. Prepare rice according to package directions. Preheat oven to 350° (176° C). Mix all ingredients and ¼ cup (60 ml) water. Pour into sprayed 11 x 7-inch or 9 x 9-inch (28 x 18 or 23 x 23 cm) baking dish. Cover and bake 25 minutes or until mixture bubbles and heats through.

Yield: About 8 cups
Calories: 183
Fat: 4 g
Calcium: 41 mg
Sugar Alcohol: 0 g

Serving size: 1 cup (240 ml)
Protein: 14 g   Carbohydrate: 22 g
Cholesterol: 31 mg   Sodium: 424 mg
Fiber: 1 g   Sugars: 1 g
Food Exchanges: 1½ lean meat, 1 bread, ½ other carb

Outdoor Fizzy Chicken

Net Carbs: 7 g

1 (2 to 3 pound) whole fryer, trimmed	**1.5 - 2 kg**
2 tablespoons Mrs. Dash® Chicken Grilling Blend,	
divided	**30 ml**
1 (12 ounce) can reduced-carb cola or diet cola	**340 g**
1½ cups Carb Options™ barbecue sauce	**360 ml**

1. Rub inside cavity of chicken with 1½ teaspoons (7 ml) seasoning. Coat outside of chicken with non-stick cooking spray.

2. Pour out ½ can cola and make 2 to 3 additional holes in can top. Spoon remaining seasoning into cola can. With chicken held upright, place chicken cavity on cola can, pulling legs out to form a tripod.

3. Light 1 side of grill and preheat to medium.

4. Set chicken upright on grill away from direct heat source. Cover with grill lid and cook about 1 hour or until chicken turns golden and registers 180° (80° C) when meat thermometer is inserted in leg or breast.

5. Let stand 5 minutes and serve with barbecue sauce.

Tip: Be sure to trim all fat and skin from chicken for the most nutritious dish.

Yield: 4 to 6 servings	Serving size: ½ chicken breast or 1 leg plus 2 tablespoons (30 ml) barbecue sauce

Calories: 183	Protein: 24 g	Carbohydrate: 7 g
Fat: 6 g	Cholesterol: 74 mg	Sodium: 418 mg
Calcium: 11 mg	Fiber: 0 g	Sugars: 4 g
Sugar Alcohol: 0 g	Food Exchanges: 3½ lean meat, ½ other carb	

> *One small chicken thigh, 1/2 cup (120 ml) tuna or 1/2 cup (120 ml) cottage cheese are equivalent to 2 ounces (57 g) meat.*

Chicken with Sugar Snap Peas

Net Carbs: 4 g

1(16 ounce) package frozen sugar snap peas	.5 g
1 (8 ounce) package mushrooms, cleaned, sliced	227 g
2 boneless, skinless chicken breasts, cooked, cut into thin strips	
⅓ cup Sweet and Sour Sauce (p. 141)	80 ml

1. Cook sugar snap peas according to package instructions. Immediately rinse in cool water to stop cooking, drain and set aside.

2. In sprayed large skillet over medium heat, cook and stir mushrooms 5 to 6 minutes or until mushrooms are tender.

3. Add peas, chicken strips and Sweet and Sour Sauce and stir until mixture heats through. Season to taste with salt substitute and pepper.

4. Serve immediately.

Optional: Sprinkle with 1 tablespoon (15 ml) toasted sesame seeds.

Yield: 8 servings   Serving size: 1 cup (240 ml)

Calories (without sauce): 71   Protein: 11 g   Carbohydrate: 6 g
Fat: 1 g   Cholesterol: 21 mg   Sodium: 110 mg
Calcium: 42 mg   Fiber: 2 g   Sugars: 3 g
Sugar Alcohol: 0 g

Food Exchanges: 1½ lean meat, ½ vegetable

> *Thaw frozen foods in refrigerator or in the microwave, never at room temperature, which allows unsafe bacterial growth.*

Low-Carb Chicken Fajitas

Net Carbs: 14 g

1 cup sliced yellow or white onion	240 ml
1 cup green or red bell peppers, cut in strips	240 ml

1 oven-broiled or charcoal-grilled boneless, skinless chicken breast, cut in strips

4 low-carb whole wheat tortillas

1. Preheat oven to 300° (148° C).

2. In sprayed large skillet, cook and stir onions and bell peppers over medium heat until they are slightly brown and tender. Add chicken breast strips and heat. Season to taste with salt substitute and pepper.

3. Seal tortillas in aluminum foil and warm in oven about 5 minutes. To use microwave oven, place damp towels between tortillas and heat on high power only 5 to 6 seconds.

4. Transfer ingredients to serving platter and serve immediately.

Optional: Add 1 garlic clove, minced, to onion and peppers. Provide toppings such as light or fat free sour cream, salsa and/or Wakka-Moley (p. 25).

Yield: 4 servings   Serving size: 1 fajita

Calories: 178	Protein: 17 g	Carbohydrate: 15 g
Fat: 5 g	Cholesterol: 21 mg	Sodium: 664 mg
Calcium: 12 mg	Fiber: 1 g	Sugars: 3 g
Sugar Alcohol: 0 g		

Food Exchanges: 2 lean meat, 1 bread, ½ vegetable

> *To make green pepper strips or slices, hold the pepper upright on a cutting surface. Slice each of the sides from the pepper stem and discard stem, white membrane and seeds. You should have 4 large, flat pieces of pepper that are easy to slice or chop.*

Chicken-Cheese Quesadillas

Net Carbs: 5 g

2 large boneless, skinless chicken breasts, cut into strips
1½ cups seasoning blend
    (onion, peppers, celery, parsley)   **360 ml**
8 (8 inch) low-carb whole wheat tortillas   **8 (20 cm)**
1 cup shredded reduced-fat cheddar cheese   **240 ml**

1. In sprayed non-stick skillet over medium heat, cook chicken strips until meat is no longer pink. During cooking, add seasoning blend and cook and stir until onions are tender. Reduce heat to low.

2. Transfer chicken to cutting board and dice. Return chicken to skillet and mix with seasoning blend. Season to taste with salt substitute and pepper.

3. On each of 4 tortillas, spoon ¼ chicken mixture. Top with cheese and cover with another tortilla.

4. Spray skillet again with cooking spray. In batches, cook each quesadilla on both sides until tortillas brown, spraying liberally with cooking spray as needed. Keep cooked quesadillas warm.

5. Cut each quesadilla into 4 wedges and serve with light sour cream and salsa.

Yield: 8 servings (16 quesadilla wedges)   Serving size: 2 wedges

Calories: 210   Protein: 20 g   Carbohydrate: 8 g
Fat: 12 g   Cholesterol: 42 mg   Sodium: 561 mg
Calcium: 202 mg   Fiber: 3 g   Sugars: less than 1 g
Sugar Alcohol: 0 g

Food Exchanges: 1 fat, 1 medium fat meat, ½ bread

■ ■ ■

❧ Chicken-Cream Cheese Burrito

Net Carbs: 8 g

1 (8 inch) low-carb whole wheat tortilla	**20 cm**
1 tablespoon reduced-fat cream cheese (Neufchatel)	**15 ml**
1 to 2 tablespoons chopped cooked chicken breast	**15 - 30 ml**
2 teaspoons chopped green onions with tops	**10 ml**

1. Preheat oven to 400° (202° C).

2. Spread cream cheese near edge of tortilla. Add chicken and green onion. Roll tortilla and place seam side down on sprayed baking sheet.

3. Spray tortilla with cooking spray and heat 5 to 6 minutes or until cream cheese melts and tortilla browns slightly.

Optional: Serve with 1 tablespoon (15 ml) salsa.

Yield: 1 burrito

Calories: 160	Protein: 9 g	Carbohydrate: 19 g
Fat: 5 g	Cholesterol: 16 mg	Sodium: 382 mg
Calcium: 21 mg	Fiber: 11 g	Sugars: less than 1 g
Sugar Alcohol: 0 g		

Food Exchanges: 1 medium fat meat, 1 bread

■ ■ ■

Black Bean Quesadillas

Net Carbs: 6 g

1 cup canned black beans, drained, rinsed	240 ml
1 cup mild or medium salsa, divided	240 ml
12 (8 inch) low-carb whole wheat tortillas	12 (20 cm)
1 cup reduced-fat cheddar, jack or mozzarella cheese	240 ml

1. In mixing bowl, mash beans with fork and combine with ¼ cup (60 ml) salsa.

2. Spray tortillas on both sides with non-stick cooking spray. Spoon bean mixture on 6 tortillas, spreading almost to edges. Sprinkle with cheese and top with remaining tortillas.

3. Preheat sprayed griddle or skillet over medium heat until hot. Place 1 quesadilla on griddle and cook 2 to 3 minutes or until it begins to brown. Turn and cook 1 to 2 minutes.

4. Repeat with remaining quesadillas. Cut each into 6 wedges and serve hot with remaining salsa.

Optional: Add ¼ cup (60 ml) chopped green onion with tops and 3 tablespoons (45 ml) finely chopped cilantro to bean mixture.

Variation: Substitute pinto beans for black beans.

Yield: 12 servings   Serving size: 3 to 4 wedges

Calories: 133 g   Protein: 11 g   Carbohydrate: 15 g
Fat: 7 g   Cholesterol: 14 mg   Sodium: 361 mg
Calcium: 202 mg   Fiber: 9 g   Sugars: less than 1 g
Sugar Alcohol: 0 g

Food Exchanges: 1 medium fat meat, 1 bread, ½ vegetable

■ ■ ◣

Crunchy Turkey Slaw

Net Carbs: 7 g

1 cup diced and cooked turkey or chicken breasts	240 ml
1 (10 ounce) package angel-hair cabbage slaw or	
5 cups finely shredded green cabbage	280 g
1 cup sliced celery	240 ml
3 tablespoons Soy Sauce Dressing (p. 144)	
or oil and vinegar	45 ml

1. In large bowl, lightly toss turkey or chicken, cabbage and celery.

2. Cover and chill before serving.

3. Just before serving, drizzle with Soy Sauce Dressing and toss lightly. Serve immediately.

Optional: Sprinkle salad with 1 tablespoon (15 ml) toasted sesame seeds, toasted slivered almonds or toasted crushed ramen noodles before serving.

Variation: Substitute ½ cup (120 ml) sliced, rinsed water chestnuts for celery.

Yield: 6 servings   Serving size: 1 cup (240 ml)

Calories (without dressing): 52   Protein: 4 g   Carbohydrate: 9 g
Fat: less than 1 g   Cholesterol: 5 g   Sodium: 85 mg
Calcium: 37 mg   Fiber: 2 g   Sugars: 2 g
Sugar Alcohol: 0 g

Food Exchanges: ½ lean meat, ½ vegetable

■ ■ ■

Turkey Burgers

Net Carbs: 4

½ cup finely chopped onion	**120 ml**
2 slices low-carb wheat bread	
1 (1 pound) package ground turkey breast	**.5 kg**
1 cup grated zucchini	**240 ml**

1. In sprayed skillet over medium heat, cook and stir onions until tender, adding few drops water if needed. Remove from skillet and set aside.

2. In food processor or blender, process bread until crumbs are fine. (Breadcrumbs should measure 1 cup/240 ml.)

3. In mixing bowl, lightly mix onion, breadcrumbs, turkey and zucchini. Season to taste with salt substitute and pepper.

4. Form mixture into 5 to 6 patties. In sprayed skillet over medium heat, place patties and cook 3 to 4 minutes on each side. Do not overcook or meat will be dry.

Yield: 5 to 6 patties   Serving size: 1 patty

Calories: 207	Protein: 24 g	Carbohydrate: 6 g
Fat: 10 g	Cholesterol: 74 mg	Sodium: 147 mg
Calcium: 31 mg	Fiber: 2 g	Sugars: 2 g
Sugar Alcohol: 0 g		

Food Exchanges: 3 lean meat, ½ bread

Vegetarian products such as soy burgers contain processed soybean protein, also known as textured vegetable protein.

Spaghetti and Meatballs

Net Carbs: 11 g

1 (12 ounce) package frozen Italian-style turkey meatballs	340 g
1 (12 ounce) package reduced-carb spaghetti	340 g
1 (8 ounce) package fresh mushrooms, sliced	227 g
3 cups Homemade Spaghetti Sauce (p. 141) or 3 cups Carb Options™ garden-style sauce	710 ml

1. Heat meatballs according to package directions for baking in conventional or microwave oven.

2. While meatballs are heating, prepare spaghetti according to package directions.

3. In sprayed skillet over medium heat, cook and stir mushrooms 5 minutes or until tender.

4. Combine mushrooms, meatballs and pasta sauce. Serve 1 meatball and ¼ cup (60 ml) sauce with ½ cup (120 ml) cooked spaghetti.

Yield: 12 servings   Serving size: 1 meatball with pasta and sauce

Calories (without sauce): 162   Protein: 14 g   Carbohydrate: 18 g
Fat: 3 g   Cholesterol: 22 mg   Sodium: 314 mg
Calcium: less than 1 mg   Fiber: 7 g   Sugars: 1 g
Sugar Alcohol: 0 g

Food Exchanges: 1 bread, ½ lean meat

■ ■ ■

❧ Delicious Low-Carb Lasagna

Net Carbs: 4 g

4 to 6 zucchini squash, cut in lengthwise slices	
1 (1 pound) ground turkey breast	**.5 kg**
2 cups Carb Options™ garden-style sauce	**480 ml**
1 cup shredded reduced-fat mozzarella or jack cheese	**240 ml**

1. Preheat oven to 350° (176° C) .

2. In large skillet or Dutch oven, heat ½ cup (120 ml) water until it boils. Reduce heat. Add zucchini, reduce heat, cover and simmer until zucchini is clear and tender. Drain and set aside.

3. Spray dry skillet with cooking spray and add ground turkey. Cook and stir until turkey turns white.

4. Add pasta sauce and ¼ cup (60 ml) water. Simmer 15 to 20 minutes to blend flavors.

5. In sprayed 9 x 13-inch (23 x 33 cm) baking dish, place zucchini in single layer. Pour meat sauce over zucchini. Cover and bake 15 to 20 minutes or until mixture bubbles and heats through.

6. Uncover and sprinkle with cheese. Return to oven 5 minutes or until cheese melts.

Variation: Substitute 1 (1 pound/.5 kg) package lean ground beef for turkey. Drain fat from meat and skillet before adding pasta sauce.

Yield: About 10 servings   Serving size: ¾ to 1 cup (180 - 240 ml)

Calories: 117   Protein: 15 g   Carbohydrate: 6 g
Fat: 4 g   Cholesterol: 23 mg   Sodium: 315 mg
Calcium: 90 mg   Fiber: 2 g   Sugars: 3 g
Sugar Alcohol: 0 g

Food Exchanges: 2 lean meat, 1 other carb, ½ vegetable

■ ■ ■

Turkey or Chicken Teriyaki Packet

Net Carbs: 4 g

2 (5 x 4 x ¼ inch) turkey steaks or
    2 boneless, skinless chicken breast halves   **2 (13 x 10 cm)**
1 cup sliced fresh mushrooms, divided   **240 ml**
½ red bell pepper, slivered, divided
2 tablespoons Carb Options™ Asian teriyaki marinade 30 ml

1. Preheat oven to 350° (176° C).

2. On each of 2 large pieces aluminum foil, place turkey steaks and season to taste with pepper.

3. Top each with ½ cup (120 ml) sliced mushrooms and ¼ cup (60 ml) red pepper. Spoon on 1 tablespoon (15 ml) marinade.

4. Fold aluminum foil to make tight seal around turkey and vegetables.

5. Bake 15 minutes. Remove from oven and spoon sauce on mushrooms and peppers. Reseal and bake another 10 to 15 minutes or until vegetables are tender and turkey is white and tender.

6. Serve in opened packets or transfer turkey, vegetables and sauce to dinner plate.

Yield: 2 servings   Serving size: 1 packet

Calories: 221   Protein: 35 g   Carbohydrate: 5 g
Fat: 12 g   Cholesterol: 86 mg   Sodium: 582 mg
Calcium: 32 mg   Fiber: 1 g   Sugars: 3 g
Sugar Alcohol: 0 g

Food Exchanges: 5 lean meat

Baking, roasting, outdoor grilling, and oven broiling are some of your best methods for low fat cooking of meat, poultry and fish.

Turkey Meatballs Carbonara

Net Carbs: 4 g

1 (12 ounce) package frozen Italian-style turkey meatballs	340 g
1 yellow or white onion, thinly sliced	
4 slices turkey bacon, cut into pieces	
1 (1 pound) jar Carb Options™ alfredo sauce	.5 kg

1. Follow package directions for heating meatballs in conventional or microwave oven.

2. In sprayed large skillet, cook and stir onion and bacon until onion is tender and bacon cooks. (Spray skillet again if needed.)

3. Mix ⅓ cup (80 ml) water and alfredo sauce. Add to skillet with onion and bacon. Bring to boil and reduce heat to simmer. Add cooked meatballs and heat through.

Optional: Serve each meatball with ¼ cup (60 ml) sauce over ⅓ cup (80 ml) cooked reduced-carb pasta.

Yield: 12 meatballs   Serving size: 1 meatball with sauce

Calories: 139   Protein: 6 g   Carbohydrate: 5 g
Fat: 10 g   Cholesterol: 44 mg   Sodium: 529 mg
Calcium: 2 mg   Fiber: 1 g   Sugars: less than 1 g
Sugar Alcohol: 0 g

Food Exchanges: 1 fat, ½ bread, ½ high fat meat, ½ vegetable

*The sharpness of white onions and red onions can
be reduced by storing in the refrigerator.*

ᥰ **Roasted Cornish Hens with Fresh Orange Relish**

Net Carbs: 14 g

2 (1¼ to 1½ pound) frozen cornish hens	2 (.7 - .8 kg)
2 oranges	
¼ cup dried cranberries or raisins	60 ml
1 tablespoon chopped pecans	15 ml

1. Thaw hens according to package instructions. Preheat oven to 450° (230° C). Rinse hens and pat dry inside and outside with paper towels.

2. Spray roasting pan and hens with non-stick cooking spray. Season hens with salt substitute and pepper to taste. Place roasting pan on middle rack in oven.

3. Roast hens uncovered about 50 minutes until juices run clear when a wood pick or fork is inserted in meaty part of the hen or when an inserted meat thermometer registers 180° (80° C).

4. While hens roast, prepare orange relish. Grate 2 teaspoons (10 ml) orange peel, remove peel, separate into sections and cut in ½-inch (1.2 cm) pieces.

5. In small bowl, combine orange pieces, dried cranberries and pecans. Transfer to serving dish and sprinkle orange peel on top. Cover and chill until serving time.

6. When ready to serve, cut hens in half lengthwise. Serve with fresh orange relish.

Yield: 4 servings   Serving size: ½ hen and ¼ cup (60 ml) relish

Calories: 407	Protein: 30 g	Carbohydrate: 16 g
Fat: 3 g	Cholesterol: 168 mg	Sodium: 84 mg
Calcium: 53 mg	Fiber: 2 g	Sugars: 11 g
Sugar Alcohol: 0 g		

Food Exchanges: 3 fat, 1 medium fat meat, 1 fruit

*One-fourth cup of dried fruit, a whole small fresh fruit, or
1/2 cup canned fruit are all equal to one fruit exchange.*

Turkey Sausage and Cabbage

Net Carbs: 9 g

1 large onion, chopped	
2 carrots, sliced	
6 cups coarsely shredded cabbage	**1.5 L**
1 (14 ounce) package smoked turkey sausage,	
** sliced in bite-size pieces**	**396 g**

1. In large sprayed Dutch oven, cook and stir onion and carrots until onion is tender.

2. Add cabbage and sausage and cook covered 15 to 20 minutes, stirring frequently, until cabbage is tender. Season to taste with salt substitute and pepper.

Optional: Add 1 garlic clove, minced. Garnish with 1 tablespoon (15 ml) toasted pine nuts.

Yield: 6 servings   Serving size: 1 cup (240 ml)

Calories: 135   Protein: 12 g   Carbohydrate: 12 g
Fat: 6 g   Cholesterol: 41 mg   Sodium: 611 mg
Calcium: 48 mg   Fiber: 3 g   Sugars: 6 g
Sugar Alcohol: 0 g

Food Exchanges: 1½ medium fat meat, 1 other carb, ½ vegetable

Bite-size—cut into pieces about 1 inch (2.5 cm) in size.

Shrimp-Avocado Feast

Net Carbs: 2 g

1 head romaine or leaf lettuce

2 ripe avocados

1 pound cooked, peeled, veined shrimp	**.5 kg**
4 tablespoons Lemon Oil Dressing (p. 144)	**60 ml**

1. With knife, cut out large lettuce ribs or stems. Roll lettuce and hold while cutting in ¼-inch (.6 cm) pieces. Pile lettuce on 4 salad plates.

2. Halve each avocado and remove seed. With peel still on, cut each half into 4 wedges. With fingers, carefully pull peel away. Arrange wedges on lettuce.

3. Arrange shrimp on top of avocado. Drizzle each plate with 1 tablespoon (15 ml) dressing and serve immediately.

Yield: 4 servings   Serving size: 1½ cups (360 ml)

Calories (without dressing): 212   Protein: 17 g   Carbohydrate: 9 g
Fat: 13 g   Cholesterol: 0 mg   Sodium: 551 mg
Calcium: 84 mg   Fiber: 7 g   Sugars: 2 g
Sugar Alcohol: 0 g

Food Exchanges: 1½ fat, ½ medium fat meat, ½ vegetable

■ ■ ■

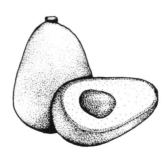

❧ Shrimp Florentine

Net Carbs: 3 g

2 (10 ounce) bags fresh spinach, rinsed	**2 (280 g)**
2 to 3 teaspoons corn starch	**10 - 15 ml**
2 pounds frozen cooked, peeled, veined shrimp	**1 kg**
Lemon-pepper seasoning to taste	

1. In sprayed large skillet, cook spinach 3 to 5 minutes over medium heat or until it is limp.

2. Mix corn starch with 2 to 3 teaspoons (10 - 15 ml) water and stir until it dissolves. Add corn starch mixture to skillet, bring to boil and stir until it thickens.

3. Add shrimp and seasoning. Reduce heat to low and cook until shrimp heats through.

4. Serve immediately.

Yield: 8 servings   Serving size: About 1 generous cup (240 ml)

Calories: 140   Protein: 25 g   Carbohydrate: 4 g
Fat: 2 g   Cholesterol: 172 mg   Sodium: 313 mg
Calcium: 130 mg
Dietary Fiber: 1 g   Sugars: 0 g
Sugar Alcohol: 0 g

Food Exchanges: 3½ very lean meat

■ ■ ■

Speedy Shrimp Creole

Net Carbs: 7 g

1 (16 ounce) package frozen seasoning blend	
(onions, celery, peppers, parsley)	**.5 kg**
1 cup sliced fresh mushrooms	**240 ml**
1 (14½ ounce) can diced tomatoes	**396 g**
1 pound fresh shrimp, peeled, veined	**.5 kg**

1. In large skillet over medium heat, cook and stir seasoning blend, mushrooms and ¼ cup (60 ml) water until vegetables are tender and liquid evaporates. Add tomatoes with liquid and simmer 15 to 20 minutes.

2. Add shrimp and cook about 10 minutes more or until shrimp turn pink and are tender. Season to taste with salt substitute and pepper.

3. Serve immediately.

Tip: You may substitute 1 (16 ounce/.5 kg) package frozen peeled, veined shrimp.

Optional: Add few dashes hot pepper sauce.

Yield: About 6 to 8 servings   Serving size: ½ cup (120 ml)

Calories: 110   Protein: 14 g   Carbohydrate: 8 g
Fat: 1 g   Cholesterol: 98 mg   Sodium: 246 mg
Calcium: 53 mg   Fiber: 1 g   Sugars: 5 g
Sugar Alcohol: 0 g

Food Exchanges: 2 very lean meat, ½ vegetable

■ ■ ■

❧ Crawfish Spaghetti Sauce

Net Carbs: 5 g

Serve this sauce over cooked reduced-carb spaghetti.

1 (10 ounce) can diced tomatoes and green chiles	**280 g**
1 (1 pound) package frozen cleaned,	
peeled crawfish tails	**.5 kg**
1 (10 ounce) can Campbell's® Healthy Request®	
cream of chicken condensed soup	**280 g**
½ (15 ounce) jar light processed cheese spread	**196 g**

1. In skillet over medium heat, heat tomatoes.

2. Add crawfish and cook and stir 10 minutes.

3. Add soup and cheese and mix well. Season with salt substitute and pepper to taste.

4. Serve over cooked pasta.

Tip: You may substitute diced tomatoes with Italian herbs for a different flavor. They are both good.

Yield: 12 servings   Serving size: About ½ cup (120 ml)

Calories (without pasta): 85   Protein: 74 g   Carbohydrate: 5 g
Fat: 3 g   Cholesterol: 65 mg   Sodium: 492 mg
Calcium: 9 mg   Fiber: less than 1 g   Sugars: 2 g
Sugar Alcohol: 0 g

Food Exchanges: 3 very lean meat, ½ vegetable

◆

To test doneness of cooked pasta, lift a piece and quickly bite into it. It should be tender, but still firm or al dente (to the tooth).

Salmon Patties

Net Carbs: 9 g

1 (12 ounce) can salmon	**340 g**
⅓ cup finely chopped onion	**80 ml**
¼ cup Egg Beaters® egg substitute	**60 ml**
11 multigrain or reduced-fat saltine crackers, crushed	

1. Drain and clean salmon of excess skin. Flake with fork. Stir in onion, egg substitute and about ¼ cup (60 ml) cracker crumbs.

2. Pack salmon mixture for each patty into ⅓ measuring cup. Flatten slightly and coat with crushed crackers.

3. Preheat non-stick skillet over high heat. Liberally spray 1 side of each patty with cooking spray. Place patty-sprayed side down in skillet. Reduce heat to medium.

4. Cook each patty for 3 minutes, spray top side of patty and turn carefully with spatula. Cook 2 to 3 more minutes or until patty turns golden brown.

5. Transfer each patty to serving plate and keep warm until all patties cook.

Yield: 6 servings (6 patties)   Serving size: 1 patty

Calories: 129	Protein: 12 g	Carbohydrate: 9 g
Fat: 4 g	Cholesterol: 20 mg	Sodium: 434 mg
Calcium: 11 mg	Fiber: less than 1 g	Sugars: 2 g
Sugar Alcohol: 0 g		

Food Exchanges: ½ bread, ½ lean meat, ½ fat

■ ■ ■

Low-Fat Tuna Melt

Net Carbs: 13 g

1 (6 ounce) can solid white albacore tuna in water, drained	168 g
2 tablespoons light mayonnaise	30 ml

8 slices low-carb wheat bread
4 slices fat-free sharp cheddar cheese

1. Preheat sprayed skillet over medium heat.

2. With fork in small mixing bowl, break up tuna into smaller flakes. Add mayonnaise and mix well.

3. On 4 slices of bread, spread tuna mixture and top with cheese and additional bread.

4. Place 1 sandwich in sprayed skillet and cook on one side until it browns. Spray top side of sandwich with cooking spray and cook that side until it browns.

5. Repeat with remaining 3 sandwiches. Serve warm.

Optional: Serve each sandwich with 1 large dill pickle.

Yield: 4 sandwiches   Serving size: 1 sandwich

Calories: 195   Protein: 30 g   Carbohydrate: 17 g
Fat: 4 g   Cholesterol: 23 mg   Sodium: 873 mg
Calcium: 2 mg   Fiber: 4 g   Sugars: 3 g
Sugar Alcohol: 0 g

Food Exchanges: 1 bread, 1 very lean meat, ½ fat

■ ■ ■

Green Chili Sauce

Net Carbs: 3 g

1 tablespoon regular stick margarine or butter	**15 ml**
1½ tablespoons flour	**22 ml**
1½ cups Swanson® Natural Goodness™ chicken broth	**360 ml**
1 (4.5 ounce) can chopped green chiles, undrained	**124 g**

1. In heavy saucepan over medium heat, melt margarine. Add flour and stir until flour and butter mix well. When mixture bubbles, continue to cook and stir 1 minute.

2. Gradually stir in broth and heat until it boils. Cook and stir 1 minute. Add green chiles and simmer 15 to 20 minutes.

3. Use immediately or cover and chill for later use.

Optional: Add ½ cup (120 ml) finely chopped onion and 1 finely minced garlic clove to margarine before adding flour. Add pinch ground cumin.

Yield: 1½ cups   Serving size: ¼ cup (60 ml)

Calories: 31   Protein: 1 g   Carbohydrate: 3 g
Fat: 2 g   Cholesterol: 0 mg   Sodium: 219 mg
Calcium: 16 mg   Fiber: less than 1 g   Sugars: less than 1 g
Sugar Alcohol: 0 g

Food Exchanges: ½ fat

To quickly chop an onion, slice off the stem and root ends and remove peel. Halve the onion from top to root end. Place each onion half flat side down and make 1/4-inch (.6 cm) vertical slices. Holding the vertical slices together, cut 1/4-inch (.6 cm) horizontal slices. There you go!

Red Chili Enchilada Sauce

Net Carbs: 4 g

1 onion, finely chopped

2 cloves garlic, finely minced or pressed

3½ cups no-salt tomato sauce   **830 ml**

2 to 4 tablespoons chili powder, divided   **30 - 45 ml**

1. In sprayed large saucepan over medium heat, cook and stir onion and garlic 2 to 3 minutes or until onion is clear and tender.

2. Add tomato sauce and heat until it boils. Gradually stir in 2 tablespoons (30 ml) chili powder.

3. Reduce heat and simmer 15 minutes. Add additional chili powder to taste. Continue simmering at least 15 minutes, and season to taste with salt substitute.

4. Serve sauce as is or strain through wire mesh strainer. For smoother sauce, puree in food processor or blender. Refrigerate or freeze in small amounts for later use.

Optional: Add ½ teaspoon (2 ml) ground cumin and ¼ teaspoon (1 ml) crushed dried oregano.

Yield: 12 servings (About 3 cups/710 ml)   Serving size: ¼ cup (60 ml)

Calories: 31	Protein: 2 g	Carbohydrate: 6 g
Fat: less than 1 g	Cholesterol: 0 mg	Sodium: 35 mg
Calcium: 30 mg	Fiber: 2 g	Sugars: 5 g
Sugar Alcohol: 0 g	Food Exchanges: ½ vegetable	

■ ■ ■

Homemade Spaghetti Sauce

Net Carbs: 6 g

1 (12 ounce) package frozen seasoning blend	
(onions, celery, peppers, parsley)	**340 g**
2 cloves garlic, finely minced or pressed	
3 cups no-salt tomato sauce	**710 ml**
2 teaspoons Italian herb seasoning blend	**10 ml**

1. In saucepan over medium heat, cook and stir seasoning blend, ¼ cup (60 ml) water and garlic until vegetables are tender.

2. Add tomato sauce and herb blend and heat until mixture boils. Reduce heat, cover and simmer 10 to 15 minutes for flavors to blend.

Yield: 12 servings (About 3 cups/710 ml)   Serving size: About ¼ cup (60 ml)

Calories: 30	Protein: less than 1 g	Carbohydrate: 6 g
Fat: 0 g	Cholesterol: 0 mg	Sodium: 29 mg
Calcium: less than 1 g	Fiber: less than 1 g	Sugars: 5 g
Sugar Alcohol: 0 g	Food Exchanges: ½ vegetable	

■ ■ ■

Sweet and Sour Sauce

Net Carbs: 2 g

½ cup Splenda® sugar substitute	**120 ml**
1 tablespoon corn starch	**15 ml**
⅓ cup rice or white wine vinegar	**80 ml**
1 tablespoon lite (reduced sodium) soy sauce	**15 ml**

1. In medium saucepan, mix sugar substitute and corn starch. Stir in ½ cup (120 ml) water, vinegar and soy sauce and mix well.

2. Over medium heat, heat mixture until it boils, stirring constantly. Boil and stir 1 minute. Use sauce immediately or refrigerate.

Yield: 10 servings (About 1 cup/240 ml)   Serving size: 1 tablespoon (15 ml)

Calories: 8	Protein: less than 1 g	Carbohydrate: 2 g
Fat: 0 g	Cholesterol: 0 mg	Sodium: 58 mg
Calcium: 1 mg	Fiber: 0 g	Sugars: less than 1 g
Sugar Alcohol: 0 g	Food Exchanges: 0	

Spicy Tomato Sauce

Net Carbs: 7 g

1 clove garlic, finely minced	
2 (8 ounce) cans no-salt tomato sauce	**2 (227 g)**
1 teaspoon dried basil, crushed	**5 ml**
½ teaspoon dried oregano, crushed	**2 ml**

1. In sprayed 1-quart (1 L) saucepan over medium heat, cook and stir garlic about 1 minute. Do not burn. Add tomato sauce, basil, oregano and salt substitute and pepper to taste. Heat mixture until it boils, then reduce heat and simmer 5 to 6 minutes. Serve over reduced-carb or whole wheat pasta.

Yield: 4 servings (2 cups/480 ml)   Serving size: ½ cup (120 ml)

Calories: 39	Protein: 1 g	Carbohydrate: 8 g
Fat: less than 1 g	Cholesterol: 0 mg	Sodium: 37 mg
Calcium: 5 mg	Fiber: 1 g	Sugars: 7 g
Sugar Alcohol: 0 g	Food Exchanges: ½ vegetable	

Good vegetable sources of vitamin C are tomatoes,
peppers, broccoli, and cauliflower.

Mustard Sauce

Net Carbs: 3 g

2 tablespoons Smart Balance® buttery spread	30 ml
2 tablespoons quick-mixing or all-purpose flour	30 ml
2 cups skim milk	480 ml
2 to 4 tablespoons dijon-style, brown or Creole mustard	30 - 60 ml

1. In saucepan over medium heat, melt buttery spread. Stir in flour and mix well.

2. Add milk, stirring constantly until mixture boils. Boil 1 minute until mixture thickens and becomes smooth.

3. Remove from heat and stir in mustard. Serve hot or warm.

Yield: 16 servings (2 cups/480 ml)

Serving size: 2 tablespoons (30 ml)

Calories: 27
Fat: 1 g
Calcium: 32 mg
Sugar Alcohol: 0 g

Protein: 2 g
Cholesterol: less than 1 mg
Dietary Fiber: less than 1 g
Food Exchanges: 0

Carbohydrate: 3 g
Sodium: 92 mg
Sugars: 2 g

■ ■ ■

Stir-Fry Cooking Sauce

Net Carbs: 3 g

4 teaspoons corn starch	20 ml
2 teaspoons lite (reduced sodium) soy sauce	10 ml
½ teaspoon ground ginger	2 ml
2 tablespoons cooking sherry or water	30 ml

In small bowl, combine all ingredients and stir until corn starch dissolves. Stir again before using.

Yield: 4 servings (about 1 cup/240 ml)

Serving size: ¼ cup (60 ml)

Calories: 18
Fat: 0 g
Calcium: 1 mg
Sugar Alcohol: 0 g

Protein: less than 1 g
Cholesterol: 0 mg
Fiber: less than 1 g
Food Exchanges: 0

Carbohydrate: 3 g
Sodium: 120 mg
Sugars: less than 1 g

Lemon Oil Dressing

Net Carbs: less than 1 g

¼ cup olive oil	60 ml
1 teaspoon grated lemon peel	5 ml
2 to 3 tablespoons lemon juice	30 - 45 ml
1 tablespoon chopped green onion with tops	15 ml
¼ to ½ teaspoon garlic powder	1 -2 ml

1. In jar or container with lid, mix or shake all ingredients until they mix well.

2. Shake again before serving.

Yield: 8 servings (about ½ cup/120 ml)

Serving size: 1 tablespoon (15 ml)

Calories: 61	Protein: less than 1 g	Carbohydrate: less than 1 g
Fat: 7 g	Cholesterol: 0 mg	Sodium: 90 mg
Calcium: 1 mg	Fiber: less than 1 g	Sugars: less than 1 g
Sugar Alcohol: 0 g	Food Exchanges: 1½ fat	

■ ■ ■

Soy Sauce Dressing

Net Carbs: less than 1 g

4 teaspoons canola, peanut or olive oil	20 ml
4 teaspoons white wine or rice vinegar	20 ml
2 teaspoons lite (reduced sodium) soy sauce	10 ml
1 teaspoon Splenda® sugar substitute	5 ml

1. In small bowl, mix all ingredients.

2. Stir well before serving.

Yield: 9 servings (About 3 tablespoons/45 ml)
Serving size: About 1 teaspoon (5 ml)

Calories: 19	Protein: less than 1 g	Carbohydrate: less than 1 g
Fat: 2 g	Cholesterol: 0 mg	Sodium: 43 mg
Calcium: less than 1 mg	Fiber: 0 g	Sugars: less than 1 g
Sugar Alcohol: 0 g	Food Exchanges: ½ fat	

■ ■ ■

Desserts

Peach Lovers' Reward

Net Carbs: 16 g

1 (.3 ounce) package sugar-free peach gelatin mix	12 g
1 (15 ounce) can sliced peaches, reserve juice	425 g
1 (4 ounce) jar pureed peaches baby food	114 g
¼ teaspoon almond extract	1 ml

1. In saucepan, heat 1 cup (240 ml) water until it boils. Add gelatin and stir until it dissolves.

2. Add juice from peaches and mix well. Stir in pureed peaches and sliced peaches and mix well. Pour into 1½-quart (1.2 L) square dish. Chill about 4 hours or until gelatin sets.

Optional: Serve with lite or fat-free whipped topping.

Yield: 4 to 6 servings
Calories: 75
Fat: less than 1 g
Calcium: 2 mg
Sugar Alcohol: 0 g
Food Exchanges: ½ fruit, ½ other carb

Serving size: ½ cup (120 ml)
Protein: 1 g
Cholesterol: 0 mg
Fiber: 1 g

Carbohydrate: 17 g
Sodium: 36 mg
Sugars: 15 g

■ ■ ■

Super Melon-Berry Sundae

Net Carbs: 19 g

1 cup crushed fresh berries or unsweetened frozen berries, slightly thawed	240 ml
1 to 2 tablespoons Splenda® sugar substitute	15 - 30 ml
4 cups cubed melon (cantaloupe, honeydew)	.9 L
2 cups low-carb vanilla ice cream	480 ml

1. In mixing bowl, gently combine berries and sugar substitute. In each of 4 dessert bowls, place melon cubes and top with ½ cup (120 ml) ice cream. Top each sundae with ¼ cup (80 ml) berries and serve immediately.

Yield: 4 servings
Calories: 175
Fat: 6 g
Calcium: 17 mg
Sugar Alcohol: 4 g
Food Exchanges: 1 fruit, 1 other carb

Serving size: 1 sundae
Protein: 4 g
Cholesterol: 25 mg
Fiber: 6 g

Carbohydrate: 29 g
Sodium: 51 mg
Sugars: 18 g

Special Kiwi Delight

Net Carbs: 11 g

3 large kiwi fruit
2 tablespoons Splenda® sugar substitute 30 ml
1 cup lite or fat-free frozen whipped topping 240 ml
⅛ teaspoon vanilla extract .5 ml

1. Peel kiwi fruit. Cut 1 kiwi fruit crosswise in half and reserve 1 half for garnish. Cut remaining kiwi fruit into chunks.

2. In blender or food processor on medium speed, blend kiwi fruit and sugar substitute until smooth.

3. In mixing bowl, lightly mix blended kiwi fruit, whipped topping and vanilla extract.

4. Into 4 parfait or stemmed glasses, spoon kiwi fruit mixture and garnish with reserved kiwi fruit slices.

5. Chill before serving.

Variations: Substitute fresh peaches, strawberries or raspberries for kiwi fruit; substitute almond extract for vanilla extract.

Yield: 4 servings   Serving size: ½ cup (120 ml)

Calories: 80   Protein: less than 1 g   Carbohydrate: 13 g
Fat: 2 g   Cholesterol: 0 mg   Sodium: 1 mg
Calcium: 23 mg   Fiber: 2 g
Sugara: 8 g
Sugar Alcohol: 0 g
Food Exchanges: 1 fruit, ½ fat

Just 1 glazed doughnut equals 2 carbohydrate and 2 fat exchanges.

Bubbly Apple Crunch

Net Carbs: 12 g

1 (20 ounce) can lite no-sugar-added apple pie filling	**624 g**
20 Murray® sugar-free vanilla wafers	
½ teaspoon ground cinnamon	**2 ml**
¼ cup chopped pecans	**60 ml**

1. Preheat oven to 300° (148° C).

2. Chop apple pie filling into small pieces.

3. Coarsely crush vanilla wafers. Stir cinnamon and pecans into crushed wafers.

4. Spray 6 ovenproof custard cups with butter-flavored, non-stick cooking spray. Spoon ¼ cup (60 ml) pie filling into each cup and sprinkle with 1 tablespoon wafer mixture. Spoon additional ¼ cup (60 ml) pie filling onto wafer mixture and top with 1 tablespoon (15 ml) wafer mixture.

5. Heat in oven at 300° (148° C) for 20 minutes or until pie filling bubbles and heats through.

Yield: 6 servings   Serving size: 1 custard cup

Calories: 108   Protein: 1 g   Carbohydrate: 16 g
Fat: 5 g   Cholesterol: 0 mg   Sodium: 35 mg
Calcium: 5.5 mg   Fiber: less than 1 g   Sugars: 6 g
Sugar Alcohol: 3 g

Food Exchanges: 1 bread, 1 fat, ½ fruit

If a can of fruit is labeled "unsweetened," it means that no sugar has been added. Keep in mind there are natural sugars in the fruit.

Maple Syrup Stir-Fry Apples

Net Carbs: 8 g

2 unpeeled tart apples, cored, thinly sliced

1 to 2 tablespoons sugar-free maple or breakfast syrup   15 - 30 ml

1. In sprayed skillet over medium heat, add apples and spray with non-stick cooking spray. Cook and stir apples until brown on both sides.

2. Add ¼ cup (60 ml) water, cover and simmer 10 to 15 minutes or until apples cook. Remove cover, increase heat to high and stir until water evaporates.

3. Serve apples warm with syrup.

Optional: If you don't want to use maple syrup, try 1 tablespoon (15 ml) Splenda® sugar substitute mixed with ½ teaspoon (2 ml) ground cinnamon.

Yield: 4 servings (about 1 cup/240 ml)   Serving size: ¼ cup (60 ml)

Calories: 37	Protein: less than 1 g	Carbohydrate: 10 g
Fat: less than 1 g	Cholesterol: 0 mg	Sodium: 2 mg
Calcium: 4 mg	Fiber: 2 g	Sugars: 7 g
Sugar Alcohol: less than 1 g		

Food Exchanges: ½ fruit

■■■

Summertime Melon Supreme

Net Carbs: 14 g

1 large lime	
4 tablespoons Splenda® sugar substitute	**60 ml**
¼ teaspoon ground ginger	**1 ml**
4 cups cubed watermelon, honeydew or cantaloupe	**.9 L**

1. Grate 1 tablespoon (15 ml) lime peel and squeeze 4 teaspoons (20 ml) fresh lime juice.

2. In saucepan, mix ½ cup (120 ml) water, lime juice, sugar substitute and ginger. Heat just until mixture begins to boil. Remove from heat and cool to room temperature.

3. Into each of 4 dessert bowls, place 1 cup (240 ml) melon cubes. Drizzle with lime juice mixture.

4. Garnish with grated lime peel and serve.

Yield: 4 servings   Serving size: 1 cup melon with syrup (240 ml)

Calories: 47
Fat: less than 1 g
Calcium: 11 mg
Sugar Alcohol: 0 mg

Protein: less than 1 g
Cholesterol: 0 mg
Fiber: less than 1 g

Carbohydrate: 14 g
Sodium: 2 mg
Sugars: 10 g

Food Exchanges: 1 fruit

■ ■ ■

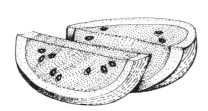

Down-Home Stewed Apples

Net Carbs: 24 g

6 firm, mildly tart Granny Smith, Gala or Jonathan apples

⅔ cup water or unsweetened apple juice   **160 ml**

2 teaspoons ground cinnamon

    or 1 large cinnamon stick   **10 ml**

2 tablespoons Splenda® sugar substitute   **30 ml**

1. Peel and core apples. Cut in ½-inch (1.2 cm) thick slices.

2. In large heavy skillet or saucepan, place apples and add water and ground cinnamon.

3. Cover and simmer, stirring frequently, over low heat about 20 minutes or until apples are tender but not mushy.

4. Stir in sugar substitute and mix until it dissolves, about 1 minute. Remove from heat. Serve warm.

Yield: About 4 servings   Serving size: ½ cup (120 ml)

Calories: 111   Protein: less than 1 g   Carbohydrate: 30 g
Fat: less than 1 g   Cholesterol: 0 mg   Sodium: 2 mg
Calcium: 27 mg   Fiber: 6 g   Sugars: 22 g
Sugar Alcohol: 0 g

Food Exchanges: 2 fruit

Many canned and bottled juices are loaded with sugar and calories. Look for "no sugar added" and "unsweetened" varieties.

Angel Pistachio-Strawberry Trifle

Net Carbs: 16 g

2 (1 ounce) packages sugar-free	
instant pistachio pudding mix	2 (28 g)
4 cups skim milk	.9 L
1 prepared strawberry sugar-free angel food cake	
3 cups sliced fresh strawberries, slightly crushed	710 ml

1. In mixing bowl, combine pudding mix and milk and mix well. Tear cake into bite-size pieces.

2. In trifle bowl or large clear glass bowl, place ⅓ cake pieces in single layer. Spoon ¼ pudding over cake, followed by 1 cup (240 ml) strawberries.

3. Repeat layers twice, ending with strawberries on top.

4. Chill before serving.

Optional: Garnish each serving with 2 tablespoons (30 ml) lite or fat-free whipped topping.

Yield: 10 to 12 servings   Serving size: ¾ cup (180 ml)

Calories: 113	Protein: 5 g	Carbohydrate: 26 g
Fat: less than 1 g	Cholesterol: 2 mg	Sodium: 463 mg
Calcium: 87 mg	Fiber: 1 g	Sugars: 6 g
Sugar Alcohol: 9 g		

Food Exchanges: 1 bread, ½ fruit, ½ milk

◆

*Store fresh strawberries in the refrigerator in
a shallow container covered with
plastic wrap. Use within 3 days.*

Guiltless Fruit Parfait

Net Carbs: 14 g

2 (6 ounce) cartons low-carb vanilla yogurt	**2 (168 g)**
1 to 3 tablespoons sugar-free fruit drink powder	**15 - 45 ml**
2 cups mixed fresh fruit*	**480 ml**
4 tablespoons lite or fat-free frozen whipped topping, thawed	**60 ml**

1. In mixing bowl, combine yogurt and drink powder to taste.

2. Into 4 parfait or stemmed glasses, layer ¼ cup (60 ml) yogurt, 2 tablespoons (30 ml) fruit, ¼ cup (60 ml) yogurt and 2 tablespoons (30 ml) fruit.

3. Top each dessert with 1 tablespoon (15 ml) whipped topping before serving.

*Tip: Strawberry and fruit punch drink powders are really good. Strawberries, apples, peaches, and blueberries are terrific. If you use fruit that browns easily such as peaches and bananas, serve immediately or sprinkle fruit with fruit preservative.

Yield: 4 servings   Serving size: 1¼ cups (300 ml)

Calories: 97	Protein: 4 g	Carbohydrate: 16 g
Fat: less than 1 g	Cholesterol: 0 mg	Sodium: 61 mg
Calcium: 9 mg	Fiber: 2 g	Sugars: 10 g
Sugar Alcohol: 0 g		

Food Exchanges: ½ fruit, ½ skim milk

■ ■ ■

 *Desserts*

❦ White Chocolate-Strawberry Trifle

Net Carbs: 16 g

2 (1 ounce) packages sugar-free instant white chocolate pudding mix	2 (28 g)
4 cups skim milk	.9 kg
4 cups sliced fresh strawberries	.9 kg
1 (8 ounce) carton frozen strawberry Whipped topping, thawed	227 g

1. In mixing bowl, combine pudding mix and milk and mix well.

2. In 2-quart (2 L) glass bowl or trifle bowl, spread 2 cups (480 ml) pudding and 2 cups (480 ml) sliced strawberries. Repeat layers. Spoon strawberry whipped topping on top. Serve immediately or chill.

Yield: 10 to 12 servings
Calories: 125
Fat: 4 g
Calcium: 117 mg
Sugar Alcohol: 0 g
Serving size: ½ cup (120 ml)
Protein: 3 g
Cholesterol: 0 mg
Fiber: 1 g
Food Exchanges: 1 fat, ½ fruit, ½ milk
Carbohydrate: 17 g
Sodium: 291 mg
Sugars: 9 g

Chilled Cappuccino Parfait

Net Carbs: 21 g

1 (1 ounce) package sugar-free instant vanilla pudding mix	2 (28 g)
½ cup strong brewed regular or decaffeinated coffee, chilled	120 ml
1½ cups skim milk	360 ml
2 cups lite frozen whipped topping, thawed	480 ml

1. In mixing bowl, combine pudding mix, coffee and milk and mix well.

2. Into stemmed or parfait glasses, layer 1 to 2 tablespoons (15 - 30 ml) pudding and 1 to 2 tablespoons (15 - 30 ml) whipped topping. Repeat layers twice.

3. Chill before serving.

Yield: 4 servings
Calories: 145
Fat: 4 g
Calcium: 84 mg
Sugar Alcohol: 0 g
Serving size: About ½ cup (120 ml)
Protein: 3 g
Cholesterol: 2 mg
Fiber: 0 g
Food Exchanges: 1 bread, 1 fat, ½ milk
Carbohydrate: 21 g
Sodium: 480 mg
Sugars: 9 g

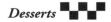

Valentine's Sweetheart Dessert

Net Carbs: 7 g

1½ cups low-carb or	
no-sugar-added strawberry yogurt	**360 ml**
1 to 2 tablespoons Splenda® sugar substitute	**15 - 30 ml**
Few drops red food coloring, if desired	
2 cups halved or sliced fresh strawberries	**480 ml**

1. In mixing bowl, combine yogurt and sugar substitute and mix well. If desired, add few drops red food coloring. Into 4 dessert dishes, place strawberries and spoon yogurt mixture on top.

Tip: This is very delicious with frozen unsweetened strawberries, partially thawed, if you cannot get fresh strawberries.

Yield: 4 servings
Calories: 68
Fat: 2 g
Calcium: 12 mg
Sugar Alcohol: 0 g

Serving size: ½ cup (60 ml)
Protein: 5 g   Carbohydrate: 8 g
Cholesterol: 8 mg   Sodium: 36 mg
Fiber: 1 g   Sugars: 6 g
Food Exchanges: ½ fruit, ½ fat

■■■

Angel Food Chocolate Sundae

Net Carbs: 26 g

½ prepared sugar-free unfrosted angel food cake	
1½ cups frozen lite whipped topping, thawed	**360 ml**
4 tablespoons sugar-free, fat-free chocolate syrup	**60 ml**
¾ cup chopped Russell Stover® low-carb toffee squares	
or other low-carb candy	**180 ml**

1. For each dessert, cut or tear 2½-inch (7 cm) slice from angel food cake. Place on dessert plate and mound with whipped topping.

2. Drizzle whipped topping with chocolate syrup. Spoon 2 to 3 teaspoons (10 - 15 ml) candy on top and serve immediately.

Yield: 4 servings
Calories: 228
Fat: 7 g
Calcium: 10 mg
Sugar Alcohol: 18 g

Serving size: 1 (2½ inch/7 cm) slice cake with toppings
Protein: 3 g   Carbohydrate: 44 g
Cholesterol: 5 mg   Sodium: 319 mg
Fiber: less than 1 g Sugars: 3 g
Food Exchanges: 2 bread, 1 fat, 1 other carb

Sweet Cherry Cobbler

Net Carbs: 11 g

1 (20 ounce) can lite no-sugar-added cherry pie filling	**624 g**
2 to 3 tablespoons Splenda® sugar substitute	**30 - 45 ml**
½ to 1 teaspoon almond extract	**2 - 5 ml**
1 (9 inch) refrigerated piecrust	**1 (23 cm)**

1. Preheat oven to 425° (220° C).

2. In mixing bowl, combine pie filling, sugar substitute and almond flavoring. Pour into 11 x 7 x 2-inch (28 x 18 x 5 cm) rectangular baking pan.

3. Unfold piecrust onto flat surface. Cut 4 (11 x 1-inch/30 x 2.5 cm) strips from piecrust. Arrange strips lengthwise over pie filling. Cut 4 (7 x 1-inch/18 x 2.5 cm) strips and arrange crosswise on pie filling.

4. Bake 25 minutes.

Optional: Sprinkle leftover piecrust with cinnamon and sugar (or sugar substitute) and bake with cobbler. Kids will love it!

Variation: If you like apples, try 1 (20 ounce/624 g) can lite no-sugar-added apple pie filling instead of cherry pie filling and substitute ½ to 1 teaspoon (2 - 5 ml) ground cinnamon for almond flavoring. You have another fabulous dessert.

Yield: About 10 servings   Serving size: ½ cup (120 ml)

Calories: 90	Protein: less than 1 g	Carbohydrate: 11 g
Fat: 5 g	Cholesterol: 0 mg	Sodium: 73 mg
Calcium: 1 mg	Fiber: less than 1 g	Sugars: 4 g
Sugar Alcohol: 0 g		

Food Exchanges: 1 fat, ½ bread

■ ■ ■

Holiday Pumpkin Flan

Net Carbs: 18 g

1 (3 ounce) package flan mix with caramel packet	84 g
1½ cups skim milk	360 ml
1 cup canned pumpkin	240 ml
⅛ teaspoon pumpkin pie spice	.5 ml

1. Into 4 custard cups, pour equal amounts caramel sauce.

2. In saucepan, prepare flan mix according to package directions using 1½ cups (360 ml) milk. After mixture boils, remove saucepan from heat and stir in pumpkin and pumpkin pie spice.

3. Slowly pour equal amounts of mixture into each custard cup. Chill covered 1 to 2 hours.

4. When ready to serve, use table knife to loosen custard. Invert each custard cup onto small dessert plate so caramel sauce covers custard.

Optional: Garnish each dessert with whipped topping.

Yield: 4 servings   Serving size: ½ cup (120 ml)

Calories: 84   Protein: 3 g   Carbohydrate: 19 g
Fat: less than 1 g   Cholesterol: 1 mg   Sodium: 90 mg
Calcium: 70 mg   Fiber: 1 g   Sugars: 4 g
Sugar Alcohol: 0 g

Food Exchanges, 1 milk, ½ other carb

---

*The higher the fat content of milk, the greater the
amount of saturated fat and cholesterol.*

❧ Chocolate Cookie-Crumb Delight

Net Carbs: 18 g

2 cups skim milk	**480 ml**
1 (1.5 ounce) package sugar-free	
instant chocolate pudding mix	**45 g**
1 (6.5 ounce) package Murray® sugar-free	
chocolate sandwich cookies, coarsely crushed	**174 g**
1 (8 ounce) carton lite frozen whipped topping,	
thawed	**227 g**

1. In mixing bowl, combine milk and pudding mix and stir well.

2. In bottom of 11 x 7 x 1½-inch (28 x 18 x 3 cm) rectangular glass dish, spread cookies and set aside ¼ cup (60 ml) for garnish.

3. Spoon pudding evenly over cookies.

4. Spread whipped topping over pudding and garnish with reserved cookies.

5. Cover with plastic wrap and refrigerate before serving.

Optional: *Double or triple this recipe for a crowd-pleasing favorite! To reduce net carbs, prepare with low-carb milk.*

Variation: *Substitute Murray® sugar-free shortbread cookies and butterscotch pudding mix or Murray® sugar-free vanilla wafers and banana cream pudding mix.*

Yield: 10 servings   Serving size: About ⅓ cup (80 ml)

Calories: 153   Protein: 3 g   Carbohydrate: 21 g
Fat: 7 g   Cholesterol: less than 1 mg Sodium: 215 mg
Calcium: 45 mg   Fiber: less than 1 g   Sugars: 5 g
Sugar Alcohol: 3 g

Food Exchanges: 1 bread, 1½ fat, ½ other carb

Supermarkets now carry a selection of lactose-free milk products for those who are lactose intolerant.

Old-Fashion Banana Pudding

Net Carbs: 29 g

2 (1 ounce) packages sugar-free	
instant vanilla pudding mix	**2 (2 .5 cm)**
4 cups skim milk	**.9 L**
3 bananas	
1 (6.5 ounce) package Murray® sugar-free vanilla wafers	**174 g**

1. In mixing bowl, combine pudding mix and milk and mix well.

2. Slice bananas.

3. Reserve 5 cookies for garnish and spread remaining vanilla wafers in 1 layer in 9 x 9-inch (23 x 23 cm) or 7 x 11-inch (18 x 28 cm) dish. Spoon 2 cups (480 ml) vanilla pudding over wafers and layer half banana slices over pudding.

4. Spread another layer of vanilla wafers and remaining banana slices. Spoon on remaining 2 cups (480 ml) vanilla pudding.

5. Crush reserved cookies and sprinkle over dessert. Chill 3 to 4 hours before serving.

Optional: To reduce net effective carbs, prepare with reduced-carb milk.

Yield: 8 to 10 servings   Serving size: ½ cup (120 ml)

Calories: 203	Protein: 6 g	Carbohydrate: 36 g
Fat: 4 g	Cholesterol: 0 mg	Sodium: 439 mg
Calcium: 135 mg	Fiber: 1 g	Sugars: 10 g
Sugar Alcohol: 6 g		

Food Exchanges: 1 bread, 1 fruit, 1 fat, ½ milk

4-Layer Chocolate Delight

Net Carbs: 15 g

½ (8 ounce) package reduced-fat cream cheese (Neufchatel)	114 g
1 (1.5 ounce) package sugar-free instant chocolate pudding mix	45 g
2 cups skim milk	480 ml
8 (2 inch square) chocolate graham crackers	8 (5 cm)

1. In mixing bowl, beat cream cheese with electric mixer or wire whisk until it is very smooth.

2. In separate bowl, combine pudding mix and milk and mix well.

3. Add pudding to cream cheese and gently stir or swirl to mix.

4. In each of 4 dessert bowls, crumble 1 chocolate graham cracker. Spoon ½ cup (120 ml) pudding mixture on crumbs. Crumble additional graham cracker on top.

5. Cover and chill before serving.

Variation: Substitute 8 Murray® sugar-free chocolate sandwich cookies for graham crackers.

Yield: 4 to 5 servings   Serving size: ½ cup (120 ml)

Calories: 149   Protein: 7 g   Carbohydrate: 15 g
Fat: 6 g   Cholesterol: 18 mg   Sodium: 465 mg
Calcium: 144 mg   Fiber: less than 1 g   Sugars: 7 g
Sugar Alcohol: 0 g

Food Exchanges: 1 bread, 1 fat, ½ other carb

Sugar-free puddings and gelatins are an excellent and inexpensive way to satisfy a sweet tooth.

Mandarin Orange Heaven

Net Carbs: 16 g

1 (1 ounce) package sugar-free instant vanilla pudding mix	**28 g**
1½ cups skim milk	**360 ml**
½ teaspoon orange or almond extract	**2 ml**
1 (11 ounce) can mandarin oranges, drained	**312 g**

1. In mixing bowl, combine pudding mix and milk and stir well.

2. Stir in almond or orange extract.

3. Carefully fold mandarin oranges into pudding. Spoon into 4 custard cups, parfait glasses or stemmed glasses. Chill before serving.

Variation: *To use as pie filling, pour prepared pudding into 1 (6 ounce/168 g) reduced-fat graham cracker crust. Top with lite whipped topping and chill before serving.*

Yield: 4 servings   Serving size: ½ cup (120 ml)

Calories: 76   Protein: 3 g   Carbohydrate: 16 g
Fat: less than 1 g   Cholesterol: 2 mg   Sodium: 336 mg
Calcium: 90 mg   Fiber: less than 1 g   Sugars: 10 g
Sugar Alcohol: 0 g

Food Exchanges: ½ fruit, ½ milk

When counting portion sizes for canned fruit, count on the fruit with a small amount of juice.

Cherry-Almond Tapioca Crunch

Net Carbs: 20 g

1 (3 ounce) package fat-free tapioca pudding mix	84 g
2 cups skim milk	480 ml
1 (20 ounce) can lite cherry pie filling	624 g
⅓ cup slivered almonds, toasted	80 ml

1. Prepare tapioca with skim milk according to package directions. Be prepared to cook and stir mixture over medium heat about 15 minutes (have this cookbook handy to look through while you are stirring). After tapioca boils, remove from heat, let stand 15 minutes and stir twice.

2. Pour tapioca into 9 x 9-inch (23 x 23 cm) dish or into 4 individual custard cups. Cover with plastic wrap and chill about 30 minutes.

3. After tapioca thickens to pudding consistency, spoon cherry pie filling on top and sprinkle with almonds.

4. Chill again before serving.

Optional: Stir 2 to 3 tablespoons (30 - 45 ml) Splenda® sugar substitute and ½ teaspoon (2 ml) almond extract into cherry pie filling before spreading on tapioca.

Yield: 8 servings (about 4 cups/.9 L)   Serving size: ½ cup (120 ml)

Calories: 117	Protein: 3 g	Carbohydrate: 20 g
Fat: 3 g	Cholesterol: 1 mg	Sodium: 80 mg
Calcium: 70 mg	Fiber: less than 1 g	Sugars: 0 g
Sugar Alcohol: 0 g		

Food Exchanges: 1 fruit, ½ fat, ½ milk

■ ■ ■

Lemon Meringue Pudding Cups

Net Carbs: 17 g

¼ cup corn starch	60 ml
1½ cups Splenda® sugar substitute, divided	360 ml
2 eggs, separated	
2 tablespoons fresh lemon juice	30 ml

1. Preheat oven to 350° (176° C).

2. In saucepan over medium heat, mix corn starch and 1¼ cups (300 ml) sugar substitute. Gradually stir in 1½ cups (360 ml) cold water and stir until smooth.

3. Slightly beat egg yolks and stir into corn starch mixture. Stirring constantly, heat mixture until it boils and continue to boil 1 minute.

4. Remove from heat and stir in lemon juice and dash salt. Spoon into 4 ovenproof custard cups.

5. With electric mixer at high speed, beat 2 egg whites. When whites foam, gradually add ¼ cup (60 ml) sugar substitute and beat until soft white peaks form. Mound meringue in peaks on top of pudding.

6. Bake at 350° (176° C) for 15 minutes or until meringue turns golden brown.

Yield: 4 servings   Serving size: 1 custard cup (120 ml)

Calories: 69   Protein: 3 g   Carbohydrate: 17 g
Fat: 2 g   Cholesterol: 106 mg   Sodium: 36 mg
Calcium: 14 mg   Fiber: less than 1 g   Sugars: less than 1 g
Sugar Alcohol: 0 g

Food Exchanges: 1 bread

■ ■ ■

ઢ **Pumpkin Pie In-A-Flash**

Net Carbs: 12 g

This is so easy for a pie or pudding. Bake a 9-inch (23 cm) prepared piecrust for this quick recipe or pour filling into 8 custard cups for a pudding dessert.

1 cup canned pumpkin puree	**240 ml**
3 cups skim milk	**710 ml**
2 (.9 ounce) packages sugar-free	
cook-and-serve vanilla pudding mix	**2 (25 g)**
1 teaspoon pumpkin pie spice	**5 ml**

1. Measure pumpkin to have ready before cooking pudding.

2. In heavy medium saucepan over medium heat, pour milk and stir in pudding mix and pumpkin pie spice. Cook over medium heat, stirring constantly, until mixture comes to full boil. Mixture will be thick.

3. Remove from heat and immediately stir in pumpkin.

Optional: For garnish, top pudding with mixture of 1½ cups (360 ml) lite frozen whipped topping and ½ teaspoon (2 ml) orange extract or 1 teaspoon (5 ml) finely grated orange peel.

Yield: 8 servings   Serving size: ⅛ of pie

Calories: 61   Protein: 3 g   Carbohydrate: 12 g
Fat: less than 1 g   Cholesterol: 2 mg   Sodium: 151 mg
Calcium: 93 mg   Fiber: less than 1 g   Sugars: 10 g
Sugar Alcohol: 0 g

Food Exchanges: ½ bread

◆

In this recipe, be sure to use regular canned pumpkin, not pumpkin pie mix, which contains added sugar.

Toffee Candy Pie

Net Carbs: 10 g

1 (8 ounce) carton lite frozen whipped topping, thawed	227 g
1 (1 ounce) package sugar-free instant butterscotch pudding mix	28 g
2½ cups low-carb vanilla ice cream, softened	600 ml
3 (1 ounce) packages Russell Stover® low-carb toffee squares, frozen, coarsely chopped	3 (28 g)

1. In mixing bowl, combine whipped topping and pudding mix.

2. Add ice cream and mix well.

3. Reserve about 1 tablespoon (15 ml) chopped candy for garnish and fold remaining candy into pudding mix.

4. Spoon pie into 1 (6 ounce/168 ml) graham cracker crust, garnish with reserved candy and freeze.

5. Remove pie from freezer about 10 minutes before serving.

Yield: 8 servings (1 pie)   Serving size: ⅛ pie

Calories (without crust): 178   Protein: 2 g   Carbohydrate: 21 g
Fat: 10 g   Cholesterol: 19 mg   Sodium: 191 mg
Calcium: 0 mg   Fiber: 3 g   Sugars: 4 g
Sugar Alcohol: 8 g

Food Exchanges: 2 fat, 1½ other carb

*Low-carb candies and chocolates are a
special treat now widely available.
Remember to watch portion sizes and calories.*

Lime Cheesecake You'll Love

Net Carbs: 9 g

2 cups low-fat small curd cottage cheese	480 ml
1 (8 ounce) package reduced-fat cream cheese	
(Neufchatel)	227 g
1 cup Splenda® sugar substitute	240 ml
3 to 4 limes	

1. In wire mesh strainer over large bowl, spoon cottage cheese and set in refrigerator to drain 30 minutes.

2. Preheat oven to 350° (176° C) and remove upper oven rack.

3. Transfer well drained cottage cheese to food processor or electric mixer, and beat until very smooth. Add cream cheese and beat again until mixture is smooth.

4. Grate 4 teaspoons (20 ml) lime peel, and squeeze 2 tablespoons (30 ml) lime juice. Add sugar substitute, 2 teaspoons (10 ml) lime peel and lime juice to cream cheese mixture. Mix thoroughly.

5. In lightly sprayed 8-inch (20 cm) springform pan, pour mixture. Place pan on large piece aluminum foil and carefully fold foil up over edges of pan so water will not leak into pan.

6. Set springform pan in large baking dish with sides and pour very hot or boiling water into baking dish until water reaches halfway up sides of springform pan.

7. Transfer pans to lower or middle oven rack and bake at 350° (176° C) for about 45 minutes or until edges of cheesecake puff, but center is still moist. Cool completely before removing from pan. Garnish with reserved lime peel and serve.

Optional: Serve with fresh crushed strawberries.

Variation: Substitute 2 teaspoons (10 ml) vanilla or almond extract for lime juice and peel.

Yield: 6 servings   Serving size: ⅙ cheesecake

Calories: 161	Protein: 13 g	Carbohydrate: 9 g
Fat: 10 g	Cholesterol: 32 mg	Sodium: 395 mg
Calcium: 85 mg	Sodium: 395 mg	
Calcium: 85 mg	Fiber: less than 1 g	Sugars: less than 1 g
Sugar Alcohol: 0 g	Food Exchanges: 1 medium fat meat	

Creamy Peanut Butter Bites

Net Carbs: 3 g

¼ cup Carb Options™ creamy peanut spread	60 ml
1½ tablespoons Splenda® sugar substitute	22 ml
1 tablespoon nonfat dry milk powder	15 ml
2 to 3 tablespoons chopped dry roasted	
unsalted peanuts	30 - 45 ml

1. In small bowl, mix peanut spread, sugar substitute and milk powder. Form mixture into 1-inch (2.5 cm) balls and add few drops water if needed. Roll balls in chopped peanuts. Serve immediately or chill.

Yield: About 10 (1 inch/2.5 cm) balls   Serving size: 2 balls

Calories: 106   Protein: 4 g   Carbohydrate: 4 g
Fat: 9 g   Cholesterol: less than 1 mg Sodium: 57 mg
Calcium: 13 mg   Fiber: 1 g   Sugars: 1 g
Sugar Alcohol: 0 g   Food Exchanges: 2 fat

■■■

Sugar-Free Cookie Piecrust

Net Carbs: 18 g

1½ cups fine crumbs of Murray® sugar-free	
vanilla wafers	360 ml
⅓ cup Smart Balance® buttery spread, melted	80 ml

1. Preheat oven to 350° (176° C). In mixing bowl, combine cookie crumbs and buttery spread and mix well. In 8-inch pie plate, pat crumbs evenly.

2. Bake at 350° (176° C) for 10 minutes, remove from oven and cool. Fill crust with no-bake pie filling of your choice. Chill as needed until pie filling sets.

Yield: 8 servings   Serving size: ⅛ crust

Calories: 229   Protein: 3 g   Carbohydrate: 28 g
Fat: 13 g   Cholesterol: 0 mg   Sodium: 199 mg
Calcium: 0 mg   Fiber: 0 g   Sugars: 0 g
Sugar Alcohol: 10 g   Food Exchanges: 2½ fat, 2 bread

Yummy Graham Cracker Piecrust

Net Carbs: 33 g

1½ cup crumbs of plain graham cracker crumbs	360 ml
2 tablespoons Splenda® sugar substitute	30 ml
⅓ cup Smart Balance® buttery spread, melted	80 ml

1. Preheat oven to 350° (176° C). In mixing bowl, combine graham cracker crumbs and sugar substitute and mix well. Stir in buttery spread and mix.

2. In 9-inch (23 cm) pie plate, pat crumbs evenly.

3. Bake at 350° (176° C) for 10 minutes, remove from oven and cool.

4. Fill crust with no-bake pie filling of your choice. Chill as needed until pie filling sets.

Yield: 8 servings   Serving size: ⅛ crust

Calories: 233   Protein: 3 g   Carbohydrate: 33 g
Fat: 10 g   Cholesterol: 0 mg   Sodium: 317 mg
Calcium: 10 mg   Fiber: less than 1 g   Sugars: 13 g
Sugar Alcohol: 0 g

Food Exchanges: 2 bread, 2 fat

■ ■ ■

Lemon-Zest Cheesecake

Net Carbs: 11 g

2 cups part-skim ricotta cheese, drained	**480 ml**
1 (8 ounce) package reduced-fat cream cheese	
(Neufchatel)	**227 g**
1 cup Splenda® sugar substitute	**240**
1 lemon	

1. Preheat oven to 350° (176° C).

2. In food processor or electric mixer, beat ricotta cheese until very smooth. Add cream cheese and beat well.

3. Grate 2 tablespoons (30 ml) lemon peel and squeeze 1 tablespoon (15 ml) lemon juice. Add sugar substitute, lemon juice and grated peel to cream cheese mixture and mix thoroughly.

4. Pour mixture into sprayed 8-inch (20 cm) springform pan. Form aluminum foil from bottom to top of pan to prevent water leaks. Place pan in larger baking dish and pour very hot or boiling water in larger dish until water reaches halfway up springform pan.

5. Place pans carefully in oven and bake 45 minutes or until cheesecake puffs slightly. Cheesecake is done when table knife is inserted into middle of cheesecake and comes out clean.

Optional: Serve with fresh crushed strawberries.

Variation: For a little different flavor, substitute 2 cups (480 ml) well drained cottage cheese for ricotta cheese. Substitute 2 teaspoons (10 ml) vanilla for lemon juice and zest.

Yield: 6 servings	Serving size: ⅙ cheesecake

Calories: 201	Protein: 13 g	Carbohydrate: 11 g
Fat: 13 g	Cholesterol: 47 mg	Sodium: 214 mg
Calcium: 266 mg	Fiber: less than 1 g	Sugars: less than 1 g
Sugar Alcohol: 0 g		

Food Exchanges: 1 medium fat meat, ½ fat

■ ■ ■

Nutty Hot Fudge Ice Cream Pie

Net Carbs: 11 g

Tastes like an old-fashion ice cream bar!

3 cups low-carb vanilla ice cream, softened	**710 ml**
1 (8 ounce) carton lite frozen whipped topping,	
thawed	**227 g**
⅓ cup chopped mixed nut ice cream topping	**80 ml**
Smuckers® Sugar-Free Hot Fudge Topping™	

1. In mixing bowl, combine ice cream and whipped topping and mix well.

2. Spoon mixture into 1 (6 ounce/168 g) graham cracker crust and sprinkle nuts evenly over top.

3. Heat hot fudge topping according to directions on jar, drizzle over pie and freeze.

4. Remove from freezer about 10 minutes before serving.

Variation: Substitute low-carb chocolate, low-carb strawberry or low-carb mint ice cream for vanilla ice cream.

Yield: 8 servings (filling for 1 pie)   Serving size: 1 slice (⅛ pie)

Calories (without crust): 186   Protein: 3 g   Carbohydrate: 18 g
Fat: 10 g   Cholesterol: 19 mg   Sodium: 40 mg
Calcium: 0 mg   Fiber: 3 g   Sugars: 5 g
Sugar Alcohol: 4 g

Food Exchanges: 2 fat, 1 other carb

◆

"Low carb" does not always been "low calorie." Check the food label.

Chocolate Cream Pie

Net Carbs: 8 g

4 ounces reduced fat-cream cheese **(Neufchatel), softened**	**114 g**
1 (1.5 ounce) package sugar-free **instant chocolate pudding mix**	**45 g**
2 cups skim milk	**480 ml**
¼ cup chopped pecans, toasted	**60 ml**

1. In mixing bowl, beat cream cheese with electric mixer or wire whisk until very smooth.

2. In separate bowl, combine pudding mix and milk and mix well.

3. Add pudding to cream cheese and gently stir or swirl to mix. Fold in pecans.

4. Spoon mixture into 1 (6 ounce/168 g) graham cracker crust.

5. Cover and chill before serving.

Optional: Top with mixture of 1½ cups (360 ml) lite whipped topping and 1 tablespoon (15 ml) miniature chocolate chips or chopped sugar-free chocolate.

Yield: 8 servings   Serving size: ⅛ of pie

Calories (without crust): 97   Protein: 4 g   Carbohydrate: 8 g
Fat: 6 g   Cholesterol: 12 g   Sodium: 242 mg
Calcium: 69 mg   Fiber: less than 1 g   Sugars: 3 g
Sugar Alcohol: 0 g

Food Exchanges: 1 fat, ½ bread, ½ milk

Peanut Butter Cup Pie

Net Carbs: 11 g

½ cup Smuckers® natural creamy peanut butter	120 ml
2 cups low-carb vanilla ice cream, softened	480 ml
1 (8 ounce) carton lite frozen whipped topping, thawed	227 g
3 (1.2 ounce) packages Russell Stover® low-carb	
peanut butter cups, frozen, coarsely chopped	3 (34 g)

1. In mixing bowl, combine peanut butter and ice cream and mix well.

2. Add whipped topping and mix.

3. Reserve about ¼ cup (60 ml) candy for garnish and fold remaining candy into peanut butter mixture.

4. Spoon pie into 1 (6 ounce/168 g) graham cracker crust, garnish with reserved candy and freeze.

5. Remove from freezer about 10 minutes before serving.

Yield: 8 servings (1 pie)   Serving size: 1 slice (⅛ pie)

Calories (without crust): 282   Protein: 7 g   Carbohydrate: 21 g
Fat: 19 g   Cholesterol: 14 mg   Sodium: 114 mg
Calcium: 0 mg   Fiber: 3 g   Sugars: 5 g
Sugar Alcohol: 7 g   Food Exchanges: 4 fat, 1½ other carb

◆

To make chopping easier, freeze chocolate bars and other chocolate candy before beginning recipe preparation.

Mom's Banana Cream Pie

Net Carbs: 12 g

1 (.9 ounce) package sugar-free instant banana cream pudding mix	25 g
1½ cups skim milk	360 ml
1 (8 ounce) carton lite frozen whipped topping, thawed, divided	227 g
2 tablespoons flaked coconut, toasted	30 ml

1. In mixing bowl, combing pudding mix and milk and mix well. Fold in 2 cups (480 ml) whipped topping and mix.

2. Pour mixture into 1 (6 ounce/168 g) graham cracker crust. Sprinkle toasted coconut on top and chill pie until pudding sets.

Yield: 8 servings
Calories (without crust): 97
Fat: 4 g
Calcium: 42 mg
Sugar Alcohol: 0 g
Serving size: 1 slice (⅛ pie)
Protein: 2 g
Cholesterol: less than 1 g
Fiber: less than 1 g
Food Exchanges: 1 fat, ½ bread
Carbohydrate: 12 g
Sodium: 153 mg
Sugars: 6 g

Chocolate Mint Ice Cream Pie

Net Carbs: 14 g

3½ cups low-carb mint chip ice cream, softened	830 ml
1 teaspoon peppermint extract	5 ml
1 (8 ounce) carton lite frozen whipped topping	227 g
8 Murray® sugar-free chocolate sandwich cookies, crushed	

1. In mixing bowl, combine ice cream and peppermint extract. Fold in whipped topping and mix well.

2. Spoon filling into 1 (6 ounce/168 g) chocolate graham cracker crust, garnish with crushed cookies and freeze. Remove from freezer about 10 minutes before serving.

Yield: 8 servings (1 pie)
Calories: 199
Fat: 12 g
Calcium: 0 mg
Sugar Alcohol: 5 g
Serving size: ⅛ pie
Protein: 2 g
Cholesterol: 22 mg
Fiber: 4 g
Food Exchanges: 2½ fat, 1 other carb, ½ bread
Carbohydrate: 23 g
Sodium: 37 mg
Sugars: 5 g

Divine Creamy Peanut Pie

Net Carbs: 13 g

1 (8 ounce) package reduced-fat cream cheese (Neufchatel)	227 g
1 cup Smuckers® natural creamy peanut butter	240 ml
½ cup Splenda® sugar substitute	120 ml
1 (8 ounce) carton lite frozen whipped topping, thawed	227 g

1. In mixing bowl, beat cream cheese until smooth. Add peanut butter and mix well.

2. Add sugar substitute and whipped topping and mix.

3. Spoon filling into 1 (6 ounce/168 g) graham cracker crust and refrigerate.

Optional: Garnish with Smuckers® Sugar-Free Hot Fudge Topping™.

Yield: 8 servings (1 pie)   Serving size: ⅛ pie

Calories (without crust): 346   Protein: 11 g   Carbohydrate: 15 g
Fat: 26 g   Cholesterol: 21 mg   Sodium: 232 mg
Calcium: 21 mg   Fiber: 2 g   Sugars: 4 g
Sugar Alcohol: 0 g

Food Exchanges: 5 fat, 1 other carb

Natural peanut butter is made without sugar or hydrogenated oils and has a thicker texture than regular peanut butter.

❧ Dreamy Pineapple Pie

Net Carbs: 31 g

1 (1 ounce) package sugar-free instant vanilla pudding mix	**28 g**
1 (15¾ ounce) can crushed pineapple with juice	**448 g**
1 (12 ounce) carton lite frozen whipped topping, thawed, divided	**340 g**
1 (6 ounce) reduced-fat graham cracker crust	**168 g**

1. In mixing bowl, combine pudding mix and pineapple with juice.

2. Fold in 1 cup (240 ml) whipped topping at a time and lightly mix. Pour mixture into graham cracker crust. Refrigerate until pudding sets.

Yield: 8 servings
Calories: 196
Fat: 7 g
Calcium: 0 mg
Sugar Alcohol: 0 g
Food Exchanges: 1 bread, 1 fruit, 1½ fat

Serving size: ⅛ of pie
Protein: less than 1 g
Cholesterol: 0 mg
Fiber: less than 1 g

Carbohydrate: 31 g
Sodium: 236 mg
Sugars: 16 g

■ ■ ■

Cherry Coke Float

Net Carbs: 2 g

Summertime Delight!

½ to ¾ cup low-carb vanilla ice cream	**120 - 180 ml**
1 (12 ounce) can diet cherry cola	**340 g**
¼ teaspoon almond extract	**1 ml**
1 maraschino cherry with stem	

1. Into tall glass, place 1 scoop ice cream and fill glass slowly with cola. Gently stir in almond flavoring. Garnish with cherry and serve immediately.

Yield: 1 serving
Calories: 100
Fat: 6 g
Calcium: 0 mg
Sugar Alcohol: 4 g
Food Exchanges: 1 fat, ½ other carb

Protein: 2 g
Cholesterol: 25 mg
Fiber: 4 g

Carbohydrate: 10 g
Sodium: 67 mg
Sugars: 2 g

Frosty Fruit Freeze

Net Carbs: 5 g

Children and adults will love this refreshing dessert!

2 cups low-fat or fat-free buttermilk	**480 ml**
½ cup Splenda® sugar substitute	**120 ml**
Grated peel from 1 lemon	
2 cups fresh fruit (strawberries, peaches, nectarines,	
blueberries, raspberries), cut in small pieces,	
reserving several pieces for garnish.	**480 ml**

1. In 12-cup 12 (240 ml) muffin pan, place paper muffin cups.

2. In mixing bowl, combine buttermilk, sugar substitute and grated lemon peel. Fold in fruit.

3. Spoon into muffin cups, placing reserved fruit pieces on top. Cover and freeze several hours or overnight.

4. Soften slightly at room temperature and peel off paper cups before serving.

Yield: 12 servings   Serving size: 1 muffin cup (about ½ cup/120 ml)

Calories: 24   Protein: 2 g   Carbohydrate: 5 g
Fat: less than 1 g   Cholesterol: 2 mg   Sodium: 43 mg
Calcium: 52 mg   Fiber: less than 1 g   Sugars: 3 g
Sugar Alcohol: 0 g

Food Exchanges: 0

■ ■ ■

Bananas Foster

Net Carbs: 15 g

3 ripe bananas, peeled

½ cup fresh orange juice plus 4 tablespoons

    grated orange peel   **120 ml**

3 tablespoons light butter   **45 ml**

½ cup brown sugar substitute   **120 ml**

1. Halve bananas lengthwise and brush with orange juice to prevent browning.

2. In large skillet over low heat, melt light butter and stir in brown sugar substitute.

3. Add bananas and remaining orange juice and cook over medium heat about 3 minutes or bananas are almost tender.

4. Sprinkle with grated orange peel.

Optional: Serve with low carb ice cream.

Yield: 6 servings   Serving size: ½ banana

Calories: 91   Protein: 1 g   Carbohydrate: 17 g
Fat: 3 g   Cholesterol: 10 mg   Sodium: 46 mg
Calcium: 12 mg   Fiber: 2 g   Sugars: 8 g
Sugar Alcohol: 0 g

Food Exchanges: 1/2 fat, 1 fruit

■■■

Chocolate-Pecan Quesadillas

Net Carbs: 3 g

4 (6 inch) low-carb tortillas	4 (168 g)
4 tablespoons reduced-fat cream cheese (Neufchatel)	60 ml
2 tablespoons sugar-free hot fudge topping	30 ml
2 tablespoons chopped pecans	30 ml

1. Spray 2 tortillas with non-stick cooking spray.

2. On plate, place tortillas sprayed side down and spread each with 2 tablespoons (30 ml) cream cheese.

3. Spread 1 tablespoon (15 ml) fudge topping over cream cheese and sprinkle 1 tablespoon (15 ml) chopped pecans on top.

4. Preheat griddle or skillet on medium heat. Place one tortilla sprayed side down in skillet. Cover with another tortilla and spray with nonstick cooking spray.

5. Heat 2 minutes on each side or until browned spots appear on bottom. Remove and keep warm while second quesadilla is prepared.

6. Cut quesadillas into 8 wedges and serve immediately.

Yield: 16 servings   Serving size: 1 wedge

Calories: 41   Protein: 1 g   Carbohydrate: 5 g
Fat: 2 g   Cholesterol: 3 mg   Sodium: 71 mg
Calcium: 3 mg   Fiber: 2 mg   Sugars: less than 1 g
Sugar Alcohol: less than 1 g   Food Exchanges: 1/2 bread, 1/2 fat

■ ■ ■

Creamy Fruit Dream

Net Carbs: 12 g

1 (8 ounce) package reduced-fat cream cheese (Neufchatel)	227 g
1 (15 ounce) can chunky mixed fruit or fruit cocktail in juice	425 g
1 cup Splenda® sugar substitute	240 ml
1 (12 ounce) carton frozen whipped topping, thawed	340 g

1. Drain fruit cocktail and reserve juice.

2. In mixing bowl, beat cream cheese and juice. Stir in whipped topping and fold in sugar substitute and fruit. Chill before serving.

Optional: Sprinkle each serving with toasted slivered almonds.

Yield: 8 to 10 servings
Calories: 129
Fat: 8 g
Calcium: 19 mg
Sugar Alcohol: 0 g

Serving size: ½ cup (120 ml)
Protein: 3 g
Cholesterol: 19 mg
Fiber: 1 g
Food Exchanges: 1½ fat, 1 fruit

Carbohydrate: 13 g
Sodium: 107 mg
Sugars: 8 g

Key Lime Pie

Net Carbs: 24 g

2 (6 ounce) cartons fat-free, no-sugar-added key lime pie yogurt	2 (168 g)
1 (3 ounce) package sugar-free lime gelatin mix	84 g
1 (8 ounce) carton lite frozen whipped topping, thawed	227 g
1 (9 inch) reduced-fat graham cracker crust	1 (23 cm)

1. In mixing bowl, combine yogurt and lime gelatin and mix well. Fold in whipped topping and spread mixture in pie crust.

2. Freeze. Remove from freezer 20 minutes before slicing.

Yield: 8 servings
Calories: 198
Fat: 8 g
Calcium: 0 mg
Sugar Alcohol: 0 g

Serving size: 1 slice
Protein: 3 g
Cholesterol: 1 mg
Fiber: less than 1 g
Food Exchanges: 1½ bread, 1½ fat

Carbohydrate: 24 g
Sodium: 183 mg
Sugars: 11 g

Grapes Fantastic

Net Carbs: 16 g

⅓ cup light sour cream	80 ml
¼ cup whipped cream cheese spread	
with cinnamon and brown sugar	60 ml
3 cups seedless grapes, washed, drained	710 ml
⅓ cup toasted slivered almonds	80 ml

1. In mixing bowl, combine sour cream and cream cheese spread and mix well.

2. In separate bowl, fold cream cheese mixture into grapes until grapes are well coated. Chill 2 hours.

3. Spoon grapes into dessert bowls and sprinkle with toasted almonds.

Yield: 6 servings   Serving size: ½ cup (120 ml)

Calories: 139   Protein: 3 g   Carbohydrate: 18 g
Fat: 7 g   Cholesterol: 11 mg   Sodium: 29 mg
Calcium: 53 mg   Fiber: 2 g   Sugars: 14 g
Sugar Alcohol: 0 g

Food Exchanges: 1 1/2 fat, 1 fruit

■ ■ ■

A

B

Index

COOKBOOKS PUBLISHED BY COOKBOOK RESOURCES, LLC

The Ultimate Cooking with 4 Ingredients
Easy Cooking with 5 Ingredients
The Best of Cooking with 3 Ingredients
Gourmet Cooking with 5 Ingredients
Healthy Cooking with 4 Ingredients
Diabetic Cooking with 4 Ingredients
4-Ingredient Recipes for 30-Minute Meals
Essential 3-4-5 Ingredient Recipes
The Best 1001 Short, Easy Recipes
Easy Slow-Cooker Cookbook
Essential Slow-Cooker Cooking
Quick Fixes with Cake Mixes
Casseroles to the Rescue
I Ain't On No Diet Cookbook
Kitchen Keepsakes/More Kitchen Keepsakes
Old-Fashioned Cookies
Grandmother's Cookies
Mother's Recipes
Recipe Keepsakes
Cookie Dough Secrets
Gifts for the Cookie Jar
All New Gifts for the Cookie Jar
Gifts in a Pickle Jar
Muffins In A Jar
Brownies In A Jar
Cookie Jar Magic
Easy Desserts
Bake Sale Bestsellers
Quilters' Cooking Companion
Miss Sadie's Southern Cooking
Classic Tex-Mex and Texas Cooking
Classic Southwest Cooking
The Great Canadian Cookbook
The Best of Lone Star Legacy Cookbook
Cookbook 25 Years
Pass the Plate
Texas Longhorn Cookbook
Trophy Hunters' Wild Game Cookbook
Mealtimes and Memories
Holiday Recipes
Little Taste of Texas
Little Taste of Texas II
Texas Peppers
Southwest Sizzler
Southwest Olé
Class Treats
Leaving Home

cookbook
resources LLC
Bringing Family And Friends To The Table

To Order: **Diabetic Cooking with 4 Ingredients**:

Please send_____ copies @ $16.95 (U.S.) each $ _____

Texas residents add sales tax @ $1.23 each $ _____

Plus postage/handling @ $6.00 (1st copy) $ _____

$1.00 (each additional copy) $ _____

Check or Credit Card (Canada-credit card only)   Total $ _____

Charge to: ❑ MasterCard or ❑ VISA

Account # _____

Expiration Date _____

Signature_____

Name _____

Address_____

City_____State_____Zip_____

Telephone (Day)_____(Evening)_____

Mail or Call:
Cookbook Resources
541 Doubletree Dr.
Highland Village, Texas 75077
Toll Free (866) 229-2665
(972) 317-6404 Fax

— —

To Order: **Diabetic Cooking with 4 Ingredients**:

Please send_____ copies @ $16.95 (U.S.) each $ _____

Texas residents add sales tax @ $1.23 each $ _____

Plus postage/handling @ $6.00 (1st copy) $ _____

$1.00 (each additional copy) $ _____

Check or Credit Card (Canada-credit card only)   Total $ _____

Charge to: ❑ MasterCard or ❑ VISA

Account # _____

Expiration Date _____

Signature_____

Name _____

Address_____

City_____State_____Zip_____

Telephone (Day)_____(Evening)_____

Mail or Call:
Cookbook Resources
541 Doubletree Dr.
Highland Village, Texas 75077
Toll Free (866) 229-2665
(972) 317-6404 Fax